"Marcie Cuff makes nature even more fun than the way you find it. This is a book about imagination and creativity—and getting dirty. The projects in *This Book Was a Tree* remind me of the dozens of ways we can all connect with the natural world on a daily basis. And since Marcie writes from the heart, you can just feel the satisfaction and even joy you'll get from connecting a little bit more with the world around you. She has ideas that everyone can try alone or with friends or family. She's going to make a lot of lives simpler, happier, and more plugged in to the world that's all around us."

—David Yarnold, President and CEO of National Audubon Society

"It really is good to get dirty, and this is a wonderful guidebook to exactly how!"

—Bill McKibben, author of *Wandering Home*

"Somewhere, in a book of advice on aging, I read a fine adage: Do something real every day. That's good advice for people of every age. From the title of the book, through all of its pages of ideas and adventures, Marcie Chambers Cuff helps us remember what's real and what makes kids and their families feel fully alive in a virtual age."

—Richard Louv, author of *Last Child in the Woods* and *The Nature Principle*

"Whether you live in a twenty-story building in the middle of the city or on a twenty-acre preserve, this beautifully illustrated book urges us all to explore the outdoors like never before. Full of fun, simple ideas and endless inspiration, Cuff's book will help all ages get creative and get connected—to nature, to the process, and to the world in which we live."

—Bernadette Noll, author of *Slow Family Living*

continued . . .

"A book that wonderfully captures the wandering and wonderment of my youth—and brings it to life again. Part project, part prose, what was destined for my eleven-year-old niece in New England has managed to linger on my desk for too long. I might even keep it for myself!"

—M. Sanjayan, lead scientist at the Nature Conservancy and TV host

"This book still is a tree: to climb, survey, and *touch* the simple wonders of nature. Marcie Chambers Cuff gives us back the physical world: Most of all, she returns it to our children."

—Adrian Higgins, garden columnist for the *Washington Post*

"*This Book Was a Tree* is full of sparks to reignite your curiosity and engagement with the natural world around you."

—Toby A. Adams, director of the Edible Academy at the New York Botanical Garden

"If we forget where we came from, we are lost. Marcie's book offers a path home and endless opportunities to learn. We love what we know, so we have to begin with the knowing, and this book can help you begin. *This Book Was a Tree* can help anyone begin to love the natural world around them and want to be part of it."

—Ellen D. Ketterson, distinguished professor of biology and executive producer of *Ordinary Extraordinary Junco*

"If orangutans, Asian elephants, and crows can improvise creative ways to interact with nature, Marcie Cuff shows us: so can we! You are very lucky that you have picked up this book. Now go get your hands dirty and have fun!"

—Melanie Choukas-Bradley, naturalist and author of *City of Trees*

"Marcie Cuff's book is a treasure! Even a diehard nature lover like me found new inspiration and ideas for getting my kid to put down the screens and come outside and explore, ask questions, and get our hands dirty while learning about this magnificent planet we share. Any parent who is frustrated by the draw of today's relentless gadgets should bring this book home."

—Annie Leonard, author and host of *The Story of Stuff*

"*This Book Was a Tree* is a strong and creative shout-out to all of us who are artists, teachers, naturalists, parents, and simply humans. This book begs us to put down our button-pushing gadgets and challenges us to reconnect to nature through pages of timeless projects, creative acts, and deep thought. From guerrilla gardening to pinhole cameras to phenology, Ms. Cuff covers it all with the expertise of a scientist and a mother. This is not another book of 'nature crafts' you can do with a paper plate or a corn husk. The introduction alone may bring you to tears with an urgent message speaking of global damage, environmental degradation, and ozone depletion. The author invites us to keep a foot in both worlds knowing that we can come to our senses through purposeful and fun exploration of the natural environment around us, no matter where we live. I applaud *This Book Was a Tree* for being a tree first and giving the author the pages to share with us the most important message of our time."

—Amy Butler, director of education for the North Branch Nature Center and founder of ECO (Educating Children Outdoors)

"It becomes obvious early on that writing *This Book Was a Tree* was a labor of love for author Marcie Chambers Cuff. The passion in her words and conviction in her messages are real, and comforting. Her message is simple: Step away from the A/V technology of the twenty-first century and go outside to experience the natural world. Overcome the inertia of home comforts and go out and get dirty, poke things with a stick (dead things, which is how all wildlife biologists get their start), look around, use that acorn between your shoulders, and become creative, think on your own. This book is not just for city folk, nor is it just for kids. It's something to be shared between parent and child, teacher and student. It belongs at home and in schools. It's projects and adventures to be shared for years and among generations."

—Michael J. Petrula, research and management biologist, Alaska Department of Fish and Game, Division of Wildlife Conservation

This Book Was a Tree

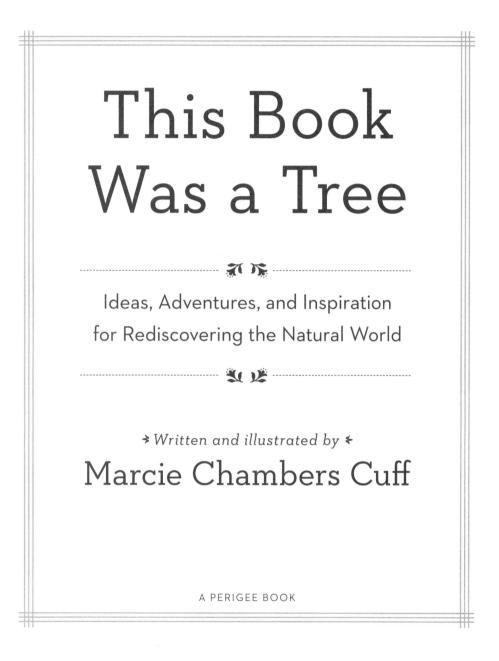

Ideas, Adventures, and Inspiration
for Rediscovering the Natural World

Written and illustrated by

Marcie Chambers Cuff

A PERIGEE BOOK

A PERIGEE BOOK
Published by the Penguin Group
Penguin Group (USA) LLC
375 Hudson Street, New York, New York 10014

USA · Canada · UK · Ireland · Australia · New Zealand · India · South Africa · China

penguin.com

A Penguin Random House Company

Library of Congress Cataloging-in-Publication Data

Cuff, Marcie Chambers.
This book was a tree : ideas, adventures, and inspiration for rediscovering the natural world /
written and illustrated by Marcie Chambers Cuff.— First edition.
pages   cm
ISBN 978-0-399-16585-6 (paperback)
1. Handicraft.   2. Nature craft.   3. Philosophy of nature.   4. Creative ability.   5. Conduct of life.
6. Frontier and pioneer life.   7. Outdoor life.   I. Title.
TT157.C77   2014
745.5—dc23   2013046446

First edition: April 2014

PRINTED IN THE UNITED STATES OF AMERICA

10   9   8   7   6   5   4   3   2   1

Text design by Tiffany Estreicher

Most Perigee books are available at special quantity discounts for
bulk purchases for sales promotions, premiums, fund-raising, or educational use.
Special books, or book excerpts, can also be created to fit specific needs.
For details, write: Special.Markets@us.penguingroup.com.

to my two small wild girls
may you always have handfuls of seeds to scatter

CONTENTS

Introduction

A funny thing happened on the way to the twenty-first century. In between uploading, replying to texts, friending and unfriending, listening to podcasts, and Googling, we all drifted off the trail. It's a complicated story, since, in many ways, our complex networked lives have mostly been improved with high-tech devices and gadgets. But, in the end, technology has displaced our exposure to the real world.

As we enter into this new frontier of *Star Trek*-like technologies, we are drifting farther down a path of massive and irreversible global damage, including environmental degradation, resource loss, water contamination, ozone depletion, and cataclysmic loss of biodiversity. If the Earth is to survive the foreseeable future, we need to reconnect with it: we need to rekindle a childlike excitement about nature and to build lasting connections that will help uncover the intrinsic value of the natural world. We need modern pioneers who see that nature is clearly valuable in and of itself.

Why? In the end, the Earth's fate depends on human attitudes and behaviors. Until we become familiar with the functioning of nature's intricate parts and can recognize the impact of our everyday actions, the outside world remains a threatened, if not endangered, species.

However well intentioned, a small book like this cannot provide a recipe for how to fix a ravaged global core. But it can dissolve the boundary between ourselves and everything else, thus nudging us gently into purposeful action. We can start by coming to our senses and trying to live lives fully engaged in the natural world—to see the relevance of wildness in itself, view ourselves as agents of change, make immediate everyday lifestyle changes based on real data, build communities around what we've learned, and spread the word. I hope this book will persuade you to reexamine your relationship with the real world and convince you to live a life that makes sense—one that contributes to a lighter, more conscious way of living on Earth.

THE MODERN PIONEER IS . . . YOU!

A pioneer is really anyone who ventures into unknown or unclaimed territory to settle. You can find traces of pioneers throughout history, in every crack and crevice of the world, within each enterprising work venture, spirited political advocacy group, or gutsy pet project. Historically, original pathmakers of all kinds attempted various passages and led hazardous expeditions through mountain ranges and up wild rivers. They laid down well-traveled routes for a second wave of settlers, and as the first pioneers slipped away over the horizon, new settlers reclaimed the land, repaired damage to existing foundations, and built upon what was already there.

While early pioneers wore battered boots and carried canteens, hatchets, and hardtack, some of today's pioneers wear crisp white lab coats and pocket protectors and stand before microscopes and blackboards to demystify the world and expound on entangled equations. But those aren't the only modern pioneers. Today, regular people like you and me—people wearing sneakers, jeans, or aprons—are making significant discoveries through everyday observation and experimentation in nature.

You are at the right place at the right time. You have stumbled upon this book and are ready to make a change. And now you—yes, *you*—are the modern pioneer. Not a leathery, backwoods deerskin-wearing salt pork and hominy sort of pioneer, or a lab-coat-wearing research type, but a strong-minded, clever, crafty, mudpie-making, fort-building pioneer. Where you stand right now was, a mere century ago, a wild frontier. Buried unwittingly beneath superhighways, vacant lots, strip malls, and vast cornfields is the old backcountry. You can still see it in places. You just have to know where to find it. And you have just discovered the tool that will help dig it up—this book.

WHO AM I TO WRITE THIS BOOK?

Success and happiness in life depends on a small number of personal qualities and accomplishments, but mostly it depends on pure luck. I was lucky enough to be born into a resourceful family that often left me to my own devices. Growing up, my brother and I spent much of our spare time exploring neighborhood thickets and forests and collecting frogs and worms. Our house was the one crammed with animals—the usual dogs, cats, gerbils, ferrets, rats, ducks, geese, raccoons, frogs, snakes, and snakelets, along with the occasional wounded wild rabbit, disoriented herring gull, and three-legged box turtle. I was the girl who built forts, waded into the pond, made mudpies, cut school to watch goslings hatch, fell victim to snakebites, and got armfuls of poison ivy. Growing up was a continuous adventure for me. Looking back, it's clear this influenced my entire life.

I learned quite early that I wanted to be some sort of science-y person. My parents were not scientists, but they were sympathetic enough to my cause to hang back and allow me to get messy. It was later on that my fascination with the outdoors and creepy-crawly things became systematized and methodical. I spent summers working as a biological field assistant, traveling to the rainforests of Mexico and Panama, the temperate forests of Virginia and Indiana, and the coral reefs of Jamaica—gathering behavioral data on monkeys, passerines, and fish, and moving from tent to cabin to weatherport. I ended up as a graduate student, living in a remote cabin and studying geese in the Alaskan tundra. While there, I began tutoring elementary school students in my free time, which sparked within me a deep appreciation for teaching the natural sciences. Eventually this triggered a cross-country move to teach biology and environmental science to those perhaps most limited by their surroundings—city kids.

That is how I developed as a scientist and teacher. Today, I'm still doing the same things, but on a different scale. Smaller, slower things. My family and I live in a suburban house atop 0.13 acres. I established a dynamic local elementary school vegetable garden, maintain a small community garden plot, shop at the weekly local farmers' market, sketch sometimes in pen and ink, and write a blog based on creative family projects and the nature behind them. For the past several years, I've been unraveling life's mysteries with my two girls. Always, their ideas propel things in an unexpected direction, and in the process, we build on an old skill, or learn a completely new one. More important, we spend time slowing down and connecting with the natural world.

Though my family is tuned in, don't imagine that I'm writing this from a passive solar geodesic dome constructed out of old freeway scraps. Our decrepit old house has drippy faucets and a tumbling composter that long ago crumbled into a fragmented pile. We have neglected soil-filled moldy pots on the back porch; shrunken, wrinkled leaves of secondhand orchids on the sill; a yellowed kitchen cactus struggling to flower year after year after year.

Much like you, I juggle the virtual and real worlds, and it's a perpetual balancing act. The rise of high-tech digital gadgets has improved my life in countless ways—helping me cook up scatter plots of Old Faithful eruptions, edit lunar cycle claymation films, and skew online bird sighting polls in my favor. I cannot pretend that I didn't spend oodles of hours in front of a screen writing this book and then send it posthaste via email attachment (in countless versions) to my editor. Within seconds it was in her hands. Quick and easy. I didn't use a pencil. I didn't use an eraser. Not even once.

I'm not here to convert you into Laura Ingalls Wilder, nor am I advocating you adopt a Davy Crockett lifestyle. Instead, I simply wish for you to cultivate a healthy relationship with the natural world here in the present.

NOW WHAT?

So, you want to be a modern pioneer. Now what?

If you're antsy like me, you'll probably pick up this book and skim it from beginning to end, discover a catchy chapter title and head straight to the mouthwatering juicy bits of an exploratory project. Do this. Absolutely. I won't tell. On the other hand, if you're patient, you'll read this book carefully from beginning to end. Regardless of how you approach it, keep this book with your bedside field guides and nature junk journal (more on these later) to reexamine periodically. Consider this book less as an acquaintance you unexpectedly run into at a mermaid convention and then abandon in the crowd, and more as a dear old neighbor that you revisit again and again with homemade banana bread—because sometimes you can read something fifty-two times and then *whammo!* on the fifty-third time the words are completely different.

This book requires interaction. Mark up its pages, take notes, provide informative thoughtful answers, sketch in its blank spaces, take it outside and get it dirty, and use it as a flower and feather press. It's all yours. You may share it. And you should. Many hands-on chapter projects may require the help of a dexterous friend or family member. Some parts of it may trigger self-reflection and quiet absorption, and some may spur wild family brainstorming.

Your world has gotten complicated. You've been handed a jumble of technological gadgets and real-life problems. You have a lot to think about. The best way to make sense of it all is to make a conscious effort to start working.

Roll up your sleeves and explore the natural world—one of unsurpassed wonder, beauty, and possibility. Decipher nature's perplexing puzzles through messy but purposeful projects—felt wool, make seedbombs, germinate sprouts, assemble a nature junk journal, maintain an herb garden, and construct a bee coop—ultimately, what I really want is for you to feel relevant and connected to nature. To reconnect and understand that you are not separate from the world, nor better than it. To observe and participate in the goings-on around you. To explore the natural world, without preconceptions. Take the time to reawaken a childlike, imaginative wonder about life, develop a deep inner relationship with nature, and then lend support to a growing environmental movement.

This is a book in which the questions considerably outnumber the answers. As you explore it, you'll be asked to look around and find solutions to everyday problems. Just do the best you can with what you've been given and don't try to do everything at once. Look around and identify a problem that needs solving, pick a few things to get done, and experiment with ecological alternatives. Every little bit helps. One small change may seem insignificant to you, but a handful of us making small changes can be powerful stuff.

PROJECT NOTES

You don't need expensive new equipment and supplies to get to know the world; you need only to have an open mind that asks good questions. All materials required for the book's projects can be found around your house or at a local thrift store, flea market, hardware store, pharmacy, or corner store.

Safety is your responsibility. Be honest with yourself in assessing whether you have the knowledge and experience needed before trying some of the book's projects. Many projects require the use of tools like utility knives, chisels, handsaws, paper cutters, and drills. If you are inexperienced, ask a skilled friend for help. Know your limitations and keep your work area neat and tidy.

Wilderness, by its very nature, is unpredictable and has inherent risk. While you are unlikely to encounter a saltwater crocodile, carpet viper, or Brazilian wandering spider when you step out your door, spending time in any kind of nature has potential hazards. With preparation and forethought, these can be minimized. Enter any wilderness properly prepared and equipped. Select appropriate clothing and equipment, don't skimp on water and snacks, and leave a detailed itinerary with someone. Avoid difficult creek crossings, stick to the trail, and know when to turn around. Give wildlife plenty of space, use care when turning over rocks or logs, and learn to recognize threatening behavior from animals and insects. A misstep while setting up a pinhole camera, a wrong turn when hiking a familiar trail—even the most sensible person can get into a real pickle when outside. To avoid misfortune, the key is to keep tabs on potential pitfalls in even the shrimpiest outing. Most important, if you run into a snag, maintain your sense of humor. Chances are, you'll return home with an impressive tale to tell.

In anticipation of the dreamy day when the entire world will share one universal measurement system, all measurements in this book are given in metric units. Despite the adoption of the metric system by 95 percent of the world and 100 percent of scientists, measuring in the United States remains chaotic. Within our inch-pound system, more than three hundred different units are used to measure various quantities. The metric system, even if it seems unfamiliar at first, will ultimately help you. It works in tens, hundreds, and thousands—not in twos, fours, eights, etc.—and is basically derived from three units—gram, meter, and liter—with mostly three prefixes—centi-, milli- and kilo-. If you're capable of shifting a decimal point, you can work with metric units. Simple as that.

GOOD LUCK!

Everything must have a beginning. And so we will begin here. Put down the phone, turn off the television and the computer, and clear your mind. Turn the page and head down a new path. Together we'll trek through the trackless wild, fight our way through countless hardships and dangers, bear the banner of change, and build a new wilderness in the republic.

There are formidable endeavors ahead of you—an off-trail hiking expedition, a clandestine small-scale planting attack, an unhygienic muddy mess, and a set of perplexing trigonometry equations. You'll need patience, courage, fortitude, tact, and presence of mind in trying times. But, soon you'll find yourself exploring in all directions, checking your compass, getting back on track, and preparing the trail for others who will come later. They're right behind you.

Now, concentrate on what is essential. Go gather up the necessary supplies along with your washboard, seeds, thread and yarn, assorted nails, shovel and pick, spices, pulley blocks, ropes, and a good sturdy tent. And prepare for the journey ahead. This is your invitation.

And so it begins.

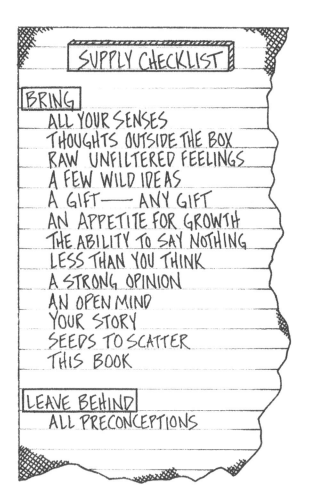

SUPPLY CHECKLIST

BRING
- ALL YOUR SENSES
- THOUGHTS OUTSIDE THE BOX
- RAW UNFILTERED FEELINGS
- A FEW WILD IDEAS
- A GIFT —— ANY GIFT
- AN APPETITE FOR GROWTH
- THE ABILITY TO SAY NOTHING LESS THAN YOU THINK
- A STRONG OPINION
- AN OPEN MIND
- YOUR STORY
- SEEDS TO SCATTER
- THIS BOOK

LEAVE BEHIND
- ALL PRECONCEPTIONS

1

Create Something

*The artist is a receptacle for emotions that come from all
over the place: from the sky, from the earth, from a scrap of
paper, from a passing shape, from a spider's web.*
—PABLO PICASSO

Once upon a time, in a land maybe not so far away, there lived a creative team of pioneers able to meet the challenges of an unpredictable wild frontier—independent visionaries determined to pursue opportunities and make lasting impacts. People who saw the world as a series of projects to be built and connections to be made. But these days, between daily thumbing and screen swiping, we've become significantly less creative.

Our progressively more complicated world requires attentive, alert, sensitive creative citizens with fresh, original ideas—people who challenge conventions and ask difficult questions—modern-day pioneers who bushwhack their own path around the world and seek knowledge for knowledge's sake. It's time to look at nature once again in a creative way. Why? Doing so will foster new connections between people and the environment. It will give rise to brand-new ideas and explanations for what lies outside your door.

Take an active role in regularly developing your natural creativity. Why? Building any sort of creative power prepares you for the moment when the world thrusts a huge problem at you. Thinking creatively helps you stray off the beaten path and come up with fresh, original ideas to approach real-world issues. Move away from looking at your environment in concrete, factual terms, and move toward considering the world in abstract, hypothetical ways. In the end, you'll gain a deep and significant relationship with the environment.

You don't have to be an artist to mess around with original ideas, craft them into their best forms, and make critical judgments along the way. Creativity is not confined to the arts—it's possible whenever you're using your brain—preparing baked Alaska, building a snow fort, or teaching advanced thermodynamics. Creativity is insight. And it's like a magic trick. First, standing before you is nothing. Then voilà! There's something new. And this new something is just amazing.

TRY THIS

The Junk Journal

If the right side of your brain has gotten flabby, it's a good idea to get your hands on something that will firm it up. A junk journal may help you sort yourself out. You'll give an old book a new lease on life, and at the same time you'll wind up with someplace to store your creative insights. Dissect an old book, transform its vintage cover, add a handful of odds and ends, and ta-da! You have a funky functional handmade journal.

PROJECT STEPS

STEP 1. Rummage through your bookshelves, poke around a thrift shop, or scour a library sale rack in search of a hardcover clothbound book on its very last legs.

STEP 2. Deconstruct the book. Open it and carefully run a craft knife in the gutter between the cover of the book and the first page. Repeat this between the cover and the last page. Remove the pages from the cover, reserving them for future projects. Take a look at the discarded pages—most likely they're comprised of stacks of folded pages, or *signatures*, glued or sewn together along one edge. The cover will now be rickety.

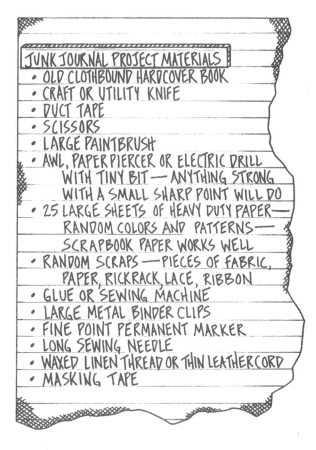

JUNK JOURNAL PROJECT MATERIALS
- OLD CLOTHBOUND HARDCOVER BOOK
- CRAFT OR UTILITY KNIFE
- DUCT TAPE
- SCISSORS
- LARGE PAINTBRUSH
- AWL, PAPER PIERCER OR ELECTRIC DRILL WITH TINY BIT — ANYTHING STRONG WITH A SMALL SHARP POINT WILL DO
- 25 LARGE SHEETS OF HEAVY DUTY PAPER — RANDOM COLORS AND PATTERNS — SCRAPBOOK PAPER WORKS WELL
- RANDOM SCRAPS — PIECES OF FABRIC, PAPER, RICKRACK, LACE, RIBBON
- GLUE OR SEWING MACHINE
- LARGE METAL BINDER CLIPS
- FINE POINT PERMANENT MARKER
- LONG SEWING NEEDLE
- WAXED LINEN THREAD OR THIN LEATHER CORD
- MASKING TAPE

STEP 3. Lay the book open with the exterior facing up. Center the duct tape on the spine lengthwise. Wrap the tape around the top and bottom spine edges overlapping tape ends on the inside to seal. Pull the tape tight and work it in with a paintbrush handle to smooth. Overlapping tape edges, place a second and third strip of tape on both sides of the first. The tape will now completely cover the binding and will extend onto the front and back book cover by 3 or 4 centimeters.

STEP 4. Open the book. Measure the cover from top to bottom (A). Measure the book from the inside edge of the front hardcover (the *hinge*) to the outside edge of the front hardcover

Which Book?

Dimensions: Cover dimensions don't matter, but the book must be fairly thick—at least 5 centimeters.

Appearance: There should be a space between the cloth spine and the bound book pages.

State of Affairs: It should be on its last legs. Though its spine should be mostly intact, it can be grungy, disheveled, and slightly damaged—in fact, the more bedraggled, the better. Choose a book that has had a full life, but is undoubtedly destined for a landfill. With luck, you'll find an unloved one past its prime with unusable moldy pages and lots of character.

(B). The book's paper height will measure A minus 1 centimeter, and the book's paper width will measure B times two minus 2 centimeters. The paper will eventually be folded in half to make fifty pages.

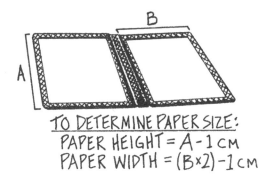

TO DETERMINE PAPER SIZE:
PAPER HEIGHT = A − 1 CM
PAPER WIDTH = (B×2) − 1 CM

STEP 5. Select twenty-five large sheets of heavy-duty paper to make the pages. Keep in mind that the paper can be mismatched in color—in fact, the quirkier the better. Cut all twenty-five sheets to the required page dimensions. Fold each sheet in half, matching B sides. Work in the crease with the paintbrush handle.

STEP 6. Now, this step is optional. Spruce up each page with random scraps. Use a threaded needle, glue, or sewing machine to attach flaps, scrap envelopes, fabric, postcards, lace, and ribbon to each page. Trim the paper edges and cut "windows" in pages for future photos.

STEP 7. Make five stacks of folded papers with five sheets of paper in each. These will be the signatures. Arrange each signature so the pages are open with all creases together in the center, like open books. Make sure the pages are even. Secure each folded signature together with a binder clip.

STEP 8. To make a hole-punching template, cut scrap cardstock the same length as the book's spine and about 5 centimeters wider. Fold the paper in half lengthwise and make a crease. With a permanent pen, mark the

Feeling Conflicted?

An old familiar book is magical and precious, like a dog-eared friend that you reach for in hard times. Spine decomposing, Post-it notes nosing out, hand-written notes in the margins—you repeatedly flip it open, then read and re-read passages from it, even complete chapters, simply because it's Just. That. Good.

A book is personal, and its value lies within its reader. There will always be a bibliophile out there worshiping even the most obscure of titles. *A Field Guide to Portable Folding Chairs*, *A History of the Tea Cozy*, *How to Sharpen a Pencil*—someone out there loves them. Because of this, judging the fate of an old book is an especially tricky thing. Only an orphaned book without personal, monetary, or historical worth should be deconstructed and given a new lease on life. You just need to visit a thrift store or local junkyard to see heaps of books simply sitting there, sadly homeless and decomposing. Mostly they deserve a good cheering up.

top of the paper on the crease. Measure the center of the crease from top to bottom and mark it with a dot. On the crease, measure successive 3-centimeter intervals above and below this central dot and mark each. Depending on book size, you will have a long series of three, five, seven, or nine dots along the crease. Draw two parallel lines 1 centimeter to the left and right of the crease, and two more parallel lines. You will have five lines, including the center crease. Mark dots on the template along each line at the same 3-centimeter intervals as the crease.

STEP 9. With the empty book binding open, set the template on the inside of the duct-taped spine. Be certain the template is exactly in the middle of the binding and that the top of the template matches the top of the book. Tape it loosely in place onto the spine with masking tape. Using an awl, sharp-pointed tool, or electric drill with a tiny bit, punch straight through each template dot into the spine. Repeat poking holes until there are five columns of holes.

STEP 10. Remove the binder clip from one signature. Open the signature up 45 degrees, align all the pages, and slip the template into the inside of the center crease, or *gutter*. Poke holes through all pages at the template dots. Repeat for each signature.

Find Your Medium

A journal may not be your thing. That's fine. But, make sure to find other ways to create. Test things out and find a language for your creative side. Grab a #2 pencil, watercolor set, Sharpie, spray paint, camera, megaphone, sousaphone, chisel, or quill, and get to work sketching, printmaking, whittling, tap dancing, or batiking. Fill canvas, fabric, graph paper, restaurant coasters, brick walls, or town halls with your stuff. You'll never know what your thing is unless you try.

STEP 11. Thread a long sewing needle with waxed linen or thin leather cord. Do not tie a knot in the end. Pass the threaded needle through the center hole of one signature all the way through into the center of the book's corresponding spine hole. Bring the needle out the exterior spine, leaving at least a 10-centimeter tail. Send the needle through the next spine and corresponding signature holes into the gutter of the book. Keep sewing a straight stitch, moving up toward the top of the spine. When you reach the hole at the spine's top, move back down, forming a figure eight with your stitches all the way to the bottom of the spine and then back toward the center. Bring thread ends to the gutter and tie them off with a square knot. Repeat this sewing for all five signatures. There will be visible stitching along the book's spine.

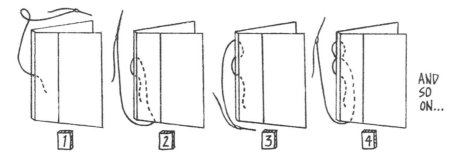

STEP 12. Decorate the cover with scrap photos, ribbon, and lace. Secure a ribbon or cord around the book for safekeeping. You're good to go!

OH, THE SCIENCE OF IT ALL!

Wild Creativity

Creativity is slippery and difficult to define. It seems, though, that one characteristic of a creative person is to be flexible when faced with a tricky situation. Really creative people can recognize or generate alternatives to the norm, and then put these alternatives to work solving problems and communicating with others. Recently, scientists have found that other animals think in ways that are considered creative—reasoning, problem solving, and crafting twigs, leaves, and feathers into simple tools. Check these out:

- ✦ Crows manufacture hooks out of discarded wire to fish grubs out of hiding places, and drop stones in glass pitchers to raise the height of water inside.
- ✦ Orangutans make improvised safety whistles from bundles of leaves, which they use to warn family members and ward off predators.
- ✦ Loggerhead shrikes use their hooked beaks to kill small vertebrates and then skewer their prey onto thorny trees or barbed wire. Often male shrikes use the impaled prey to impress nearby females with their hunting skills.
- ✦ Bottlenose dolphins carry marine sponges in their snouts to stir the sandy ocean bottom and uncover potential prey.
- ✦ Veined octopuses carry discarded coconut shell halves across the ocean floor to use later as shelters.
- ✦ Asian elephants systematically modify branches to swat at flies, breaking them down to ideal lengths for attacking the insects.
- ✦ Thread-waisted wasps hold pebbles in their jaws to hammer down soil while building nests.

✦ NOW TRY THIS ✦

Variations on a Theme

Get your creative juices flowing. Explore the world around you and start filling up your handmade junk journal with thoughts about how nature works, broad solutions to the world's problems, and dreams of what will come. Or stuff it full of self-addressed letters, fantasy planetary travel plans, ancient adages that you've creatively altered, happy thoughts while daydreaming, weird short stories you've read or plan to read, decisions to make, or risks to take. Take your pick!

Things I put in my own journal: rough sketches of honeybee dances and wingless beetles, tree bark rubbings, a list of potential inventions (snake detector, beach boots, diaper alarm, subway chin rest, and eyedropper funnel), a list of potential names for undiscovered planets, collections of useless ideas (for every stupendous one, I have ten worthless ones that may someday evolve into stupendous ones), bear fur, photos of heart-shaped rocks, and raw thoughts while sitting on tree stumps—Did you know that honeybees have hair on their eyes, slugs have four noses, and owls are the only bird that can see the color blue?

EXPLORE MORE

Creative thinking builds a deep connection between a person and the natural world. You don't need a roomful of beakers, Bunsen burners, laser cutters, injection molding equipment, or 3-D printing machines to inspire scientific creativity. Some of the most valuable creative thinking has risen from a simple spontaneous and clever merging of regular everyday things. Opportunities for discovery are all around you. Every new venture begins by addressing a problem or responding to an opportunity. At any place and any time you can look around and identify problems that need solving. And often there are resources already at your disposal to solve them. Here are more ways to get your creative juices flowing.

TAKE STUFF APART. Finding out how things tick often spurs creative thinking that can be applied to other problem solving. Grab an object

Be Safe!

Make sure the item you're taking apart is safe. Don't take apart the paper shredder. Unplug anything electric, and never disobey the safety precautions on the object you're working on. Be aware that glass, sharp things, and potentially powered electrical devices may inhabit dismantled objects.

you're willing to part with—broken alarm clock, inoperable typewriter, ruined radio, discarded doorknob, old-school wind-up toy, or disabled rotary phone—and take it apart. Disassemble it carefully. As you take it apart, see how things fit together. Keep in mind that the object may never be reassembled in perfect working condition. Experiment and explore. Test out various components to see if they work alone. Guess what each part does. Guess why each is included in the assembly. Take notes. Sketch how things fit together. Then, try to reassemble it and get it back to working order.

TAKE CAREFUL NOTES OF A DISASSEMBLED OBJECT HERE:

STEP INTO THE BOX. Creativity often thrives under rigid constraints. Many people are most creative when not given complete freedom to run reckless all over the joint. Look at poets and musicians, who often rely on literary forms and song structures with strict requirements, such as rhyme and repetition. With limited choices, ominous options are eliminated and there's little chance of a predictable outcome. You're forced to look beyond the obvious, and the outcome is something strangely original. I guess sometimes you have to step into a box to break out of it.

It's your turn to limit yourself. Make something brand-new out of something you have on hand—turn something ordinary into something extraordinary. Go outside and grab a natural object—acorn, twig, pebble, mitten-shaped leaf—and give yourself five minutes to think of as many alternative uses as possible for this object. Don't worry about practicality—let your ideas run as wild as they want.

WRITE A LONG LIST OF ALTERNATIVE USES FOR AN OBJECT RIGHT HERE:

INVENT SOMETHING. The image of doing science—making hypotheses, conducting controlled studies, and taking careful notes—is not *always* reality. Sometimes the best way to make discoveries in the world is to make small, imperfect studies—ditch the data and the hypotheses—and just try things out. Shove things around a little bit and see if anything happens. And if it does, you just may be on to something big. An original discovery can be made casually, by anyone, anywhere at any time.

Look around and see the cleverness of everyday things—like buttons, zippers, pencils, scissors, clips, and snaps. Each of these began as an inge-

nious solution to a problem, and each is ever evolving. There are always obstacles to get over or around. There are always improvements to be made. The natural world is also full of inspiration. Anything can inspire an ingenious idea.

Take a look around and identify a problem that needs solving. Combine playfulness and innovative design and come up with a wild solution to the problem. Connect ideas that don't naturally go together—an insect's antennae with an alarm clock; a maple seed with a rotary phone. Fuse mismatched totally unrelated things to create something completely original. No need for your new "something" to be functional. In fact, make something you *know* won't work. This will gear your brain up for the real stuff later on.

Don't worry about what others might think of your ingenuity. Almost every brilliant idea was horribly ridiculed and suffered a weird, lonely childhood. Almost every insightful idea has been at first perceived as ridiculous. Ignore everybody. Play around with stuff. Your creative genius could just be the next big thing.

SKETCH YOUR INGENIOUS IDEAS HERE:

UNTHINK. Sometimes *unthinking* something actually helps you *think* of something. Try it. Distance yourself from a problem you're solving—either physically or mentally. Imagine your creative task as being far away from you—as someone else's problem.

DOODLE IN THIS SPACE WHILE YOU'RE *UN*-THINKING YOUR INVENTION:

WRESTLE WITH SOMETHING. If you can't find a solution to a problem, don't give up! Sometimes solving something can take a long, long time. It's been said that after you stop searching for an answer, the answer suddenly appears and is shocking in its completeness—an uncontrollable rush of creative insight. Newton gets bonked smack-dab on the head with an apple and . . . *eureka!* He understands the universal law of gravitation. In real life, though, most innovations come in small doses after years of wrestling with a problem. Sometimes the solution is found deep in the cracks and crevices of your brain, and it takes a long while to find it.

DOCUMENT IT

Let Your Imagination Run Wild

You would tend to think that the best way to solve something would be to focus on it—to think analytically—and then to continue reworking the problem. In reality, the opposite is often better. The best place to find a creative solution to a complex, high-level problem is most likely in the woods or on a remote island where you're doing something completely unrelated. The key to creative scientific thought is to allow your mind to wander free. When scientists allow their minds to wander past their immediate research fields into places they've never been before, they often run right into their most creative insights, and *boom!* new ideas pop up.

Embracing the absurd with imaginative wondering can boost your creative thinking. It puts your mind into overdrive for a short period while you try to work out exactly what you're looking at. You imagine things you haven't actually experienced. You imagine the possibilities. Try this. Start with the far reaches of your imagination at the science fiction level, and then gradually apply constraints, such as laws of physics, experimental feasibility, and practicality.

Engage in futuristic science fantasy. Explore the consequences of a scientific innovation—something you've designed yourself, like a teleportation machine, a computer-controlled skyway, or a spider robot. Imagine a future scenario in subterranean earth in which humans dig up your invention and use it to combat or befriend aliens, mutants, or humanoid robots. Describe the scene on the next page.

SHOW YOUR IMAGINATION RUNNING RECKLESS AND WILD:

Creativity isn't really a big deal. It's not an event. It doesn't so much *happen* as it's just *allowed*. When your mind is receptive and quiet, creativity can often be cultivated. But remember this: there's never a good time to get creative. It's never easy. You must sometimes force yourself to make time for it. And often, if you make a plan and stick with it, creativity will become your habit. But mostly you need to just roll up your sleeves and start doing it.

Why? You'll gain a deep, lasting appreciation for seeking knowledge for knowledge's sake, and you'll strengthen the bond between you and the natural world. Our increasingly complex world demands a creative team of pioneers to meet its challenges. What we really need are pioneers like you with the kind of imaginative, adaptive thinking of yesteryear—independent visionaries who daydream a lot, take creativity seriously, take mental risks, and believe in things that aren't really true.

2

Change Your Perspective

*If you do not raise your eyes you will think
that you are the highest point.*
—ANTONIO PORCHIA

It's a strange and stupefying fact that while most people are completely humiliated if they've never cracked open Amis or Vonnegut, or can't recognize a Rousseau or Verdi, the same exact people feel no shame in admitting they can't identify a common backyard tree or bird.

At no time in human history have we been more disconnected with what lies outside our front doors. Within just a century, our relationship with our surroundings has transformed from one of conquest and romanticism to one of disassociation. There is a detachment from all things growing, and from knowing where things come from. In our modern culture, you can live day to day, even an entire lifetime, without considering nature. This disconnect provides an excuse to wash your hands of the whole business—to think of nature as irrelevant, and to think you're not part of the world.

In reality, you're connected to nature more intimately than you think. Most likely, just this morning you woke up in sheets made of Texas cotton, drove on tires made of African rubber trees, and drank coffee brewed with Brazilian beans. Whether you like it or not, you're utterly dependent on the environment.

It's time to reconnect with the world around you. Take a close-up view of small fragments of it. Why? To build lasting connections with our environment, you need to see the nature—the intrinsic value and realness—of everyday things. Nature is valuable in and of itself, apart from its contribution to our life and well-being. Even the smallest things have big stories to tell. The world is full of amazingness beyond your imagination—wood frogs that survive being frozen solid, beetles that can lift two hundred times their body weight, ants that herd caterpillars, and spiders that spin silk comparable to that of high-grade alloy steel. We're all equally complex and sophisticated—just evolving along different pathways.

All organisms, through a variety of signals, influence their surrounding environment. Plants and animals are not just a passive, pleasing backdrop; they are gifted manipulators with dynamic strategies and plans of their own. Each individual within a species has a personal point of view based on its own unique life experience. We all lead complicated lives filled with the pursuit of food, water, shelter, and some way to pass on our genes. We all hit stumbling blocks along the way. In fact, even a praying mantis can have trouble finding a girlfriend.

Perspective is how a situation looks from your own position and unique life experiences. It's a fluid concept. It changes over time and is dependent upon where you stand, which direction you're facing, and how closely you look at stuff. Your perspective on the world is grounded in your personal experience, which means you only see things today that have been useful to you in the past. This can create a huge problem. We've all become accustomed to walking through life simply responding to what affects only us.

To come up with new approaches to the world's problems, you must consciously look at things differently—to explore new angles, see a scene from different points of view, and increase your breadth of perspective. In this chapter, you'll build simple, powerful tools that help you expand the confines of your own perspective, broaden your outlook, and consider a range of different perspectives.

What is the value of nature? In the end, the fate of biodiversity and ecosystem health depends on human attitudes and behaviors. Until we are all once again engaged in the importance and possibilities of our surroundings from the bottom up, nature may remain a threatened, if not endangered, species. The Earth is a complicated machine. You have to understand the functioning and perspective of all of its parts to understand the entirety of the system. You have to see the Earth from different angles to understand the relevance of its wildness.

It's time to shift your way of thinking. Look at things in endlessly new and different ways. Understand the impact of your everyday decisions. Expand your bubble, let more viewpoints in, and cultivate a broader, richer form of reason that incorporates compassion for nature. Develop a broader outlook and establish a firm foundation upon which you make future decisions. Step into someone else's footprint—someone so often ignored—the centipede, the moth, and the spittlebug. Examine the world in multiple ways. See what somebody else sees.

Pinhole Camera

A pinhole camera is a simple camera without a lens. Instead, the light-tight camera housing has a very small, round hole—a *pinhole*. Light streams through the hole, projects on the back of the interior, and produces an image on a strip of film or photopaper. A pinhole camera requires practically no knowledge of photography to build or use, and can be made easily from a mix of reclaimed materials and household objects—the perfect project for anyone on a budget, curious about photography, and baffled by sophisticated light meters or interchangeable camera lenses. It is, in essence, just a black box with a teeny hole.

As simple as it may seem, this modest box with its teeny hole can bring a new perspective to the ordinary stuff of your life. A pinhole camera demands that you concentrate only on creative vision instead of complicated and expensive technology, and it provides endless options for variation and experimentation. Prized by photographers for its lack of precision, its nearly infinite depth of field, and its antique-looking, surreal one-of-a-kind images, this magical low-tech gadget draws you closer to a photograph's essence. It reminds you that art is not about capturing an image, but about becoming actively engaged in life's small moments.

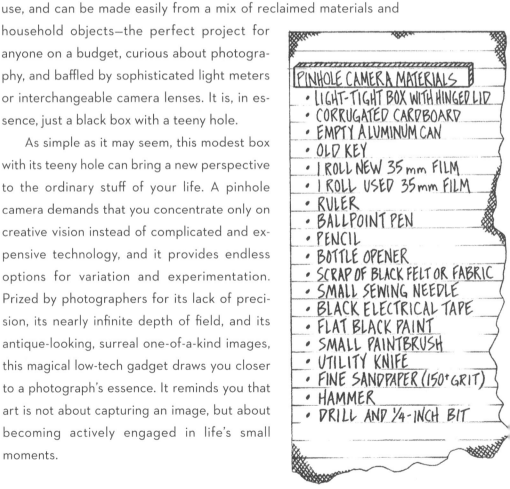

PINHOLE CAMERA MATERIALS
- LIGHT-TIGHT BOX WITH HINGED LID
- CORRUGATED CARDBOARD
- EMPTY ALUMINUM CAN
- OLD KEY
- 1 ROLL NEW 35mm FILM
- 1 ROLL USED 35mm FILM
- RULER
- BALLPOINT PEN
- PENCIL
- BOTTLE OPENER
- SCRAP OF BLACK FELT OR FABRIC
- SMALL SEWING NEEDLE
- BLACK ELECTRICAL TAPE
- FLAT BLACK PAINT
- SMALL PAINTBRUSH
- UTILITY KNIFE
- FINE SANDPAPER (150+ GRIT)
- HAMMER
- DRILL AND ¼-INCH BIT

Note: *Just about anything can serve as pinhole camera housing—a matchbox, cookie jar, cigar box, coffee can, garbage can, shoebox, or mint tin—as long as it's light-tight. I've found that a durable metal box with a hinged lid is easiest. Check your cupboards—chances are something in there will work. The box needs to be both tall and wide enough to hold two rolls of 35mm film with at least 4 centimeters of space between, measuring approximately 15 cm × 10 cm × 5 cm.*

PROJECT STEPS

STEP 1. Hold the used film cartridge vertically with the bump on the bottom. Use a bottle opener to pop off the top end. Remove the spool and film from the outer metal shell. Unwind and cut the film, leaving a 5-centimeter tail attached to the spool.

STEP 2. Turn the box upside down with the hinge facing you. On the box's underside, use a ruler and pencil to draw diagonal lines from each corner to its opposite corner. Mark the exact center of the box—where the diagonal lines meet. Place the ruler perpendicularly on the box and draw a line through the box's center. Measure down along this line 2.5 centimeters from the top. Mark with a dot. If the box is flimsy, place it over a small wooden block to provide stability. Drill a ¼-inch hole right where you've drawn the dot.

STEP 3. Turn the box on its side with the lid facing you and opening down. Drill a hole in the upper right side, 1.5 centimeters from the side and 1.5 centimeters from the open front. An old key will be used in this hole to advance the film. Place a key in the hole to check the size. The circumference of this hole must be slightly larger than that of the key. If needed, use a larger drill bit to enlarge the hole to fit the key.

STEP 4. Measure the interior height and depth of the box. Cut two pieces of corrugated cardboard the same height and depth of the box. These will be used to make internal film compartments. Place them each vertically 3 centimeters from the right and left sides of the box. Tape the cardboard into position with electrical tape. These compartments will ensure that the film cartridge and spool remain in place as the film is advanced.

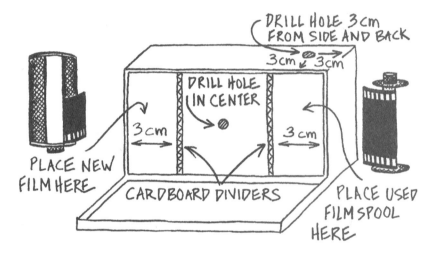

STEP 5. Turn the box on its side as in Step 3 and open the box. Remove the new film cartridge from the canister. Place the new cartridge and used spool inside the box, with the new on the left and the used on the right. To ensure a good fit, you may need to add small cardboard stacks or black scrap fabric underneath and below the cartridge and spool as spacers.

STEP 6. After you're certain of a good fit, remove the cartridge and spool and measure the inside of the box's lid (which will eventually be the

Determining Pinhole Size

Tricky mathematical equations are used to calculate perfectly precise pinhole diameters. Common formulas use the camera's focal length, the distance from the pinhole to the film at the back of the camera, the average wavelength of light, and a few other crucial numbers to determine an accurate pinhole size. Some pinholers go to great lengths to achieve the "ideal" pinhole size. Instead, I just poke a teeny tiny hole and see how it goes. Usually it all works out.

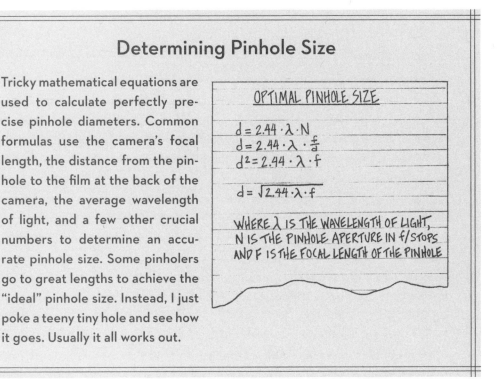

OPTIMAL PINHOLE SIZE

$$d = 2.44 \cdot \lambda \cdot N$$
$$d = 2.44 \cdot \lambda \cdot \frac{f}{d}$$
$$d^2 = 2.44 \cdot \lambda \cdot f$$

$$d = \sqrt{2.44 \cdot \lambda \cdot f}$$

WHERE λ IS THE WAVELENGTH OF LIGHT, N IS THE PINHOLE APERTURE IN f/STOPS AND f IS THE FOCAL LENGTH OF THE PINHOLE

camera's back). Cut one to three pieces of corrugated cardboard this size. Stack cardboard onto the inside of the box's lid—enough to put pressure on the film cartridge and spool to keep them in place, yet allow the film to pass from one to the other. Depending on the depth of the box, you may need to add several layers of cardboard to the lid. Everything should be nice and snug, but not tight. Glue the stacked cardboard into place.

STEP 7. Remove the spool and cartridge. Paint the entire interior of the box with flat black paint and allow it to dry overnight. Be sure that everything inside the camera is black. This will ensure that light will not reflect off any shiny surfaces. Don't paint the pinhole!

STEP 8. Cover the raw cardboard divider ends and the stacked card-

Pinhole Tips and Techniques

A pinhole camera requires a long exposure, so you're best off photographing things that aren't going anyplace. Steer clear of photographing high-speed action sports like jai alai or badminton. Portraits of toddlers may prove significantly more challenging than still objects, structures, or buildings. Find a static subject and place the camera completely still in one spot. Use something like a brick or table to steady it.

To take a photo, simply lift the pinhole flap for a certain amount of time, exposing the film, and then re-cover the pinhole. It will take some experimenting to determine exposure time (how long the flap should be open). Typically, exposure time is one to three seconds on a sunny day, three to five seconds on a cloudy day, and one to thirty minutes indoors. Determining exposure usually involves a healthy dose of guesswork. With time, you'll start to think like your camera.

Turn the key counterclockwise to advance to the next frame. It may take a few tries to determine how many rotations of the key are needed to settle on the next frame. With a good grip on how far to turn the advance, you can pack in thirty or more frames per roll. When the roll is done, take the camera into a dark closet with you, open the back, and manually slip the film back into the original film cartridge.

Pinhole camera frames are not created with the standard 35-millimeter size. Therefore, when you take the film somewhere to be processed, be sure each frame is individually marked during processing. It should not be auto cut.

board on the box's lid with black felt or black fabric scraps. This will allow the film to run smoothly from the cartridge to the spool.

STEP 9. With a utility knife, carefully cut a square piece of metal—roughly the size of a postage stamp—from a soda can. Flatten the metal piece with a hammer. Place the metal piece over a pad of paper. Press a ballpoint pen into the center of the cut metal square, creating a clearly visible dimple. Turn the metal over and thin away the bump with fine sand-paper. Poke a sewing needle's blunt end into the eraser end of a pencil. Using the point of the needle, poke a tiny hole within the metal dimple and turn the needle several times. Use sandpaper to buff the metal on both sides until smooth. Poke the needle into the hole through the opposite side and spin it several times just to be sure the hole is perfectly round. Remember: make the pinhole as tiny as possible—the smaller the pinhole, the crisper the image. Cut the stamp-sized metal down to an even smaller size—roughly 1.5 cm × 1.5 cm. Buff each side with sandpaper again. Blow through the tiny pinhole to remove any residual dust.

STEP 10. Cut a 2 cm × 2 cm piece of black electrical tape. Cut a small slit down the center. Place the electrical tape over the square pinhole metal. The tape's slit should lie around the pinhole, but should not cover the pinhole. On the inside of the box, line the pinhole up with the original drilled hole in the box's center. Secure it with electrical tape on all sides, but be certain again not to cover the pinhole.

STEP 11. Position the cartridge and spool again inside the camera. Tape the leader (the extra-skinny film end) of the new film to the remnant tail of the used spool. Insert the key through the drilled hole and into the spool. You will use the key to advance the film.

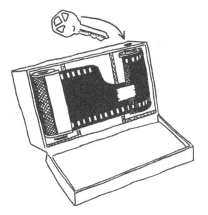

A Pinhole Mystery

You, my friend, are a visual virtuoso. Your brain devotes billions of its valuable neurons and synapses to visual intelligence. Your eyes are sophisticated supercomputers—networks of corneas, irises, retinas, and lenses—that are intimately connected to your emotional and rational intelligence.

On the other hand, the mysterious deep ocean nautilus has simple lens-less eyes with tiny pupils (1 to 2 centimeters) leading to light-sensitive cavities. Sound familiar? Pinhole camera eyes! The nautilus is the only living descendant of a group of aquatic creatures inhabiting oceans 500 million years ago when the Earth's continents were still form-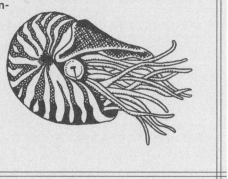ing—even older than dinosaurs. Its eyes can sense rough shapes but cannot make out any details. What's the reason behind the nautilus's poor vision? Does it hunt bioluminescent prey? Your guess is as good as mine. Its vision remains something of an enigma.

STEP 12. Make the shutter. Cut a 2 cm × 2 cm piece of electrical tape. Fold one side over halfway. This will be used as a flap. Adhere it just above the pinhole so that light cannot enter the camera.

STEP 13. Close the box's lid. You may need to tape the edges with electrical tape to ensure that no light gets into the box.

STEP 14. Turn the key counterclockwise several times to advance the film. There. Now you have yourself a camera.

OH, THE SCIENCE OF IT ALL!

Perspective Projection

When you see a scene through your own eyes, objects in the distance appear smaller than objects close by. This is known as *perspective*. The pinhole camera works on a similar principle. Each point in the scene emits light. The beams of light enter the camera through an infinitesimally small aperture (the *pinhole*). The intersection of the light rays with the image plane form the image of the object on the camera's back wall. The image is the sum of all the possible spots in the scene making corresponding dots on the film plane. Unlike you, the camera "sees" through only one single hole, resulting in a strange perspective, in many cases with scenes curving around edges. Such a mapping from three dimensions onto two dimensions is called *perspective projection*.

If you were really ambitious and were to process the film yourself in a darkroom, you'd be excited to discover that the image printed on the camera's film is inverted. As light travels toward the camera in a straight line,

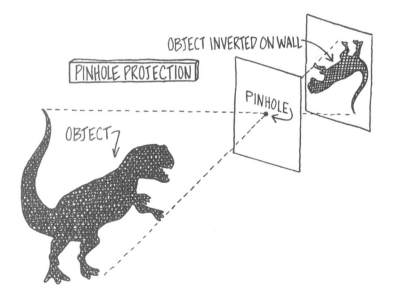

the rays coming from above enter the pinhole and strike the bottom of the camera's wall, while rays coming from below wind up at the top of the wall. After processing the film, you'd wonder, "Why doesn't the printed image have much color?" Well, the retinas in your eyes have two types of receptors: *rods* and *cones*. Rods register light and dark and are much more sensitive. Cones allow you to see color, but require more light in order to work. Since the pinhole allows only a tiny amount of light into the camera, you see the resulting image primarily with your eye's rods, and thus primarily in black and white.

Amazing what you can learn from just a black box, a teeny hole, and a piece of film. It's like seeing the world in a whole new way.

↗ NOW TRY THIS ↙

Pinhole Perspective

Put your pinhole camera to good use. This is a rare chance to put an "eye" you've built in a place you normally cannot go. Check off this list of photo sessions. Start from the top and make your way down. It may take several attempts to get things right. There will always be strange surprises. This is the appeal of pinhole photography. Celebrate the weirdness.

Pinhole Perspective Checklist

❑ Find beauty in the everyday, in the less spectacular. Photograph familiar subjects with clear graphic shapes—work boot, mug, pencil collection, wooden toy, clock, bicycle tire, or fence. Everyday life, this is where you're living. This is where things happen. Plain and honest. Look around—simple stirring subjects abound!

❏ Change your perspective without moving your feet. Stay in one place. Shift your field of view up and down, pan left and right. Experiment with different angles. Your greatest discoveries can be made by standing still.

❏ Take close-ups of delicate transitory stuff—things that don't last very long. Capture a single wildflower's bloom, dew drops on a leaf, a sprouting seed, or entangled bare branches. Get closer and closer. And then get even closer.

❏ Get a backyard bug's-eye view. Explore the way different critters see the world. Consider what life looks like through the eyes of a bird, a mole, and an aphid. Choose the locations at different eye levels in relation to natural habitats. Peek out of the underbrush, peep through foliage, peer out from behind a stump.

❏ Go elsewhere to take pictures, someplace far, far away. Capture an entire scene with depth—a grassy field, a remote winding road, a lonesome coastline, a towering cityscape. Tell a story with your camera. Look at the big picture.

❏ Fall in love with light. Notice sunlight patterns painted on a wall, light streaming through gaps in a basket, rays creeping in through tree branches. Put subjects into sunbeams. Arrange the sunny details.

❏ Capture movement. Allow the pinhole to remain open while fixed on a park or playground filled with activity. Produce a time-lapse photograph in which moving images are blurred and static images are focused. Seek contrast.

❏ Take a look at yourself. A self-portrait can be tricky, but it can be powerful. Think about who you are and what you want to say. Look at yourself from all different angles.

EXPLORE MORE

The world is different for everyone. There are possibly nine million species on earth—each with a unique perspective, and each individual within a species with a unique viewpoint on how to live life to its fullest. Your actions are based solely on how *you* view the world, on *your* perspective. The problem is that oftentimes you may fail to see the larger issues from right where you stand. To truly understand the world and see the big issues, you should view the Earth from as many points of view as you can. Develop a broader outlook. Adopting new perspectives on life requires discipline. You must constantly work at it. But you'll view the world in a brand-new way. Here are more ways to see the world differently.

CHANGE YOUR PERSPECTIVE ON SOMETHING SIMPLE. Look at an everyday thing from an ant's point of view—get down on the ground and look so close that your nose touches it. Then look at it from directly above and from below. Walk around it to the opposite side. Vary your angle of vision.

GET A BIRD'S-EYE VIEW. Take yourself out of the picture and look at where you are from way far away—as an observer, not a participant. View something familiar from a distance. Step back and look at the big picture. For example, let's pretend you're a peregrine falcon. Known for your incredibly keen vision, you're able to spot prey from an enormous height and swoop at speeds over 320 kilometers per hour. Fortunately today you are not particularly hungry since you've had your daily share of two waxwings and a field mouse and are heading back toward your precarious cliffside dwelling when you spot a collection of people below. From an elevated view, you're able to see where a supersmart person who could be reading this book lives.

Try sketching a simple map of what you see so that you may revisit it. As you draw, consider the four cardinal directions (north, south, east, west) on the map's compass rose. Get to know your surroundings. Include things that stand relatively still: the general shape of the shelter from above; major land-marks (library, school, or friendly neighborhood dogs); food supply (local market or ice cream parlor); bodies of water (lakes, rivers, or streams); but also include things that move, like public transportation (train, bus, or ferry).

SKETCH A SIMPLE MAP OF WHAT YOU SEE:

N
W — E
S

PRACTICE DISAPPEARING. Animals, and sometimes people, use all sorts of trickery to make themselves invisible to others. You can, too. Find a quiet spot. Somewhere you are comfortable. Maybe in or near the woods. Or beside a pond. Your hideout should offer enough primary cover to protect and camouflage most of you—a bush or a tree stump—and enough secondary cover (grasses, branches, or leaves) for you to look through. Lie flat, or get into a cozy seated position. Generally, the lower you are the better. Spruce yourself up with a handful of leaves or small branches to help obscure your body's outline. Blend in. Relax. Time your activity with the cycles of the wind to mask the sound of your movements—move only when the wind is moving. If you feel like shifting your body, do it slowly and quietly. Tune in. Calm your mind. Allow yourself to become part of the space you're in.

Before long, you'll notice things happening around you—a sparrow squabbling with its mate, a blue jay taunting scrambling chipmunks, a doe and fawn rambling by—even the most well-traveled spot will open up to you if you secretly become part of it. Listen to quiet things, and things you can't hear—the lone maple tree surrounded by grass, the clump of wildflowers springing from a sidewalk, the hemlock leaning clumsily on its neighbor. They know much more than you'll ever know about what it's like to be them.

DOCUMENT IT

The Rental Agreement

Although I may not think about it every day, I share my small neighborhood with thousands of outdoor critters. You do, too. Tracks and trails, rustling

RENTAL AGREEMENT

Resident: (e.g., Jumping Spider)	
Nickname: (e.g., Spidey)	
Other names used in the past: (e.g., Peter Parker)	
Length of stay on property: (e.g., spring and summer, year-round, winter, lifetime)	
Present employment: (e.g., insect wrangler, berry gatherer, leaf eater)	
Rental history: Previous home address, length of time, reason for moving: (e.g., schoolyard was too rowdy)	
Specific dietary requirements: Are foods you eat found nearby? Are foods you eat limited to one or more seasons?	
Site specifics: Does this property provide adequate food and water for you? What noises, movements, and objects soothe or frighten you?	
Purpose of your home: Will it be used for overwintering? Food storage? Rest? Protection? A hideout? A baby nursery?	
Proposed occupants: List all inhabitants in addition to yourself (nestlings, etc.)	
Effect of building: Will you build your home yourself? Will you alter the environment during home construction? (e.g., soil improvement from worm castings, flooding from a beaver dam)	
Leisure time: What do you do with most of your time? What are your sleep patterns? Will you be staying up late partying at night? Do you like the company of other animals, or prefer to live alone?	

By signing this agreement the parties hereto indicate that they have read and understood this entire agreement and agree to all of the terms, covenants, and conditions stated herein. Resident acknowledges receipt of a copy of this agreement with all addenda.

Date: _____ Guardian's Signature: _____

leaves and birdsong—all are telltale signs of mini inhabitants. Tune in, and chances are, you'll uncover clues leading you to a spiderweb, bird nest, ant mound, beetle tunnel, or insect gall.

See the world as it really is. Consider a neighbor's quality of life—a mosquito, an ant, a house mouse—any neighbor will do. Step into his or her shoes. Look at life through a lens shaped by a jumble of environmental pressures and personal experiences. Fill out a rental agreement for him or her. Consider what that critter needs to survive and thrive. You may have to think hard and do a little research to get the job done.

Few things can yield more satisfaction than exploring the natural world from different perspectives. It's the cure to human self-importance. Try it. Check things out from new angles and lenses, and voilà, you suddenly unveil the world's genius and charm. Without warning, you gain a profound sense of dependency on something much bigger than yourself—an interactive complex web of living and nonliving things. This new way of looking at the world provides a frame of reference for asking and answering important questions and evaluating the consequences of your actions. Shift your gaze. Develop a broader outlook. See the world as it really is.

3

Get Outside Every Day

*Far away there in the sunshine are my highest aspirations.
I may not reach them, but I can look up and see their beauty,
believe in them, and try to follow them.*

—LOUISA MAY ALCOTT

Besides receiving a telephone call informing you that
your long-lost hamster has been found several blocks
away from home, or getting a letter stating that your aunt
will, in fact, host Thanksgiving dinner and serve her Frog-
more Stew, one of the most delectable experiences in life is
hiking through an evergreen forest after a spring rain. The
heavy familiar smell of sunbaked soil and baby leaves—that
unmistakable fragrance you don't even realize you've missed until it
hits your brain.

Plants spend all day every day in the sun capturing light energy,
and synchronize their activity to suit regular weather variations—diverting their energies to form flowers, fruits, and seeds in spring, and protecting tender growing bits and leaves within buds in the fall. The sun

regulates and directs their major life milestones. Denied adequate sun exposure, they'll completely lose their natural twenty-four-hour rhythm. Plants have it figured out. They understand the importance of sunlight.

People today, on the other hand, have gone undercover. Being inside is safe, easy, and comfortable. It's tricky for an ordinary sun to compete with a comfy computer- or TV-filled world. We've shifted away from nature-based lifestyles to indoor-dwelling media-saturated lifestyles. And the trend continues.

Why is this a bad thing? Because light should be an integral part of life—*your* life. There's growing evidence that sun exposure is beneficial; in effect, getting yourself outside may be just as important as eating your vegetables. There's a clear and undisputed relationship between sun exposure and bone health. A mountain of new information about other health benefits include the prevention of a number of common and often fatal diseases, including heart disease, osteoporosis, multiple sclerosis, and certain types of cancers. Turns out, the sun may be as vital to your well-being as food, shelter, water, and oxygen.

Your body wasn't designed to spend so much time inside. It's time to move away from your comfort zone, escape from the virtual world, and explore wild places. Go outside every single day. Rain or shine. This chapter will prove that you don't have to be a botanist, vineyard manager, or adventure filmmaker to rediscover the wonders of the outdoors; you just have to be open to the idea that you'll have a richer, healthier, more active life if you spend some of it in the sun.

Wonderful things happen when you spend time outside. You exercise your muscles, stretch your imagination, learn new skills, tune in to the surrounding world, gain respect for natural things, and take a break from everyday stressors.

These benefits stay with you for an entire lifetime. So, let go of whatever preconceived notions you have about the sun, and go out and play. Let a little sunshine into your life.

Upcycled Terrarium

No need to be a weekend warrior with a carbon fiber kayak hitched to your bike to appreciate the out-of-doors. Getting out there doesn't require special equipment or masses of expensive gear. Instead, become reacquainted with nearby wild pockets of nature. Look around! Nature is as close as a sidewalk crack or a moss-covered stone. A handmade terrarium can remind you of this. A self-contained mini biosphere, it needs almost nothing except sunlight. You'll love the remarkable simplicity of it all; it's a daily reminder that just beyond your doorstep is a sunny world just waiting to be explored. Direct experience with nature is of utmost importance. Spending time outside challenges your mind, sharpens your focus, and staves off diseases associated with sunlight deficiency.

We're just going to jump right into the juicy bits of this project where you track down a good glass container and some small plants. Check your kitchen cabinets, backyard shed, or local thrift store. A widemouthed container is easiest—glass cloche, apothecary jar, bell jar, water jug, cookie jar, glass cube, tureen, mason jar, glass beaker, light fixture, goldfish bowl, gumball machine—and it needn't have drainage holes or a lid. In terms of size, nearly anything can work, from the tiniest jam jar on up. If you're a newbie, start with something spacious—it will provide greater options for future inhabitants and a wider margin of er-

TERRARIUM MATERIALS
- GLASS CONTAINER
  (OPEN OR CLOSED)
- CLEAN PEBBLES OR STONES
- ACTIVATED CHARCOAL BITS
- PURCHASED SHEET MOSS
- STERILE DAMP POTTING MIX
- SMALLISH PLANTS
- FUNKY FLAIR
  (SHELLS, DRIFTWOOD, OR STONES

ror. A terrarium takes just minutes to assemble—it's like making a layered taco dip. But you can't eat it.

Start fresh. Wash the container with warm soapy water. Rinse and dry it completely to remove any residue. Collect the remaining materials and head outside with them. Be prepared to get a generous dose of sunshine and get a little dirty.

TERRARIUM SPECIFICS

Topless Terrarium: Woodland Wonderland	Plant Species	Choose heat-tolerant plants like succulents: aloe, sedum, or echeveria
	Terrarium Location	Place in direct sunlight by a window
	Plant Care	Water the plants once or twice each week
Topped Terrarium: Ferns Gone Wild	Plant Species	Choose moisture-loving plants, ones that love low to medium light: mini ferns, tropical plants, mosses, or begonias
	Terrarium Location	Place in indirect light
	Plant Care	Water minimally, maybe once a month; remove lid for a few hours every two weeks to improve air circulation

PROJECT STEPS

STEP 1. Layer 1: Place an even 3- to 5-centimeter layer of clean pebbles or stones in the container. This will help absorb decaying matter within the terrarium.

STEP 2. Layer 2: Place a small handful of activated charcoal bits over the first layer.

Going Topless?

There are two types of terrariums: open and closed. An open terrarium, normally placed in direct sunlight by a window, provides a hot, dry environment for plants like succulents and cacti. A closed terrarium, or a container with a very narrow bottle-shaped mouth, acts as an independent ecological system. It provides a moist environment for plants that tolerate humidity like ferns and mosses and should receive bright indirect light. Placed directly in the sun, a closed terrarium may bake the plants. Allow the container's design to dictate its inhabitants and location.

STEP 3. Layer 3: Place a 3- to 5-centimeter layer of moss over the charcoal to prevent the soil from filtering down into the gravel.

STEP 4. Layer 4: Place a 5- to 8-centimeter layer of potting mix over the moss. Think ahead. The plant roots should not extend from the potting mix into the lower layers. Make sure there is enough depth. Gently pack the soil down to remove air pockets and level the surface.

STEP 5. Consider how you want the plants arranged. Landscape the top layer of soil with hills, valleys, mounds, or large rocks. Dig small holes into the soil where you plan to put the plants.

STEP 6. Gently tease the plant roots apart.

TERRARIUM LAYERS

SMALL PLANTS

POTTING MIX

MOSS

ACTIVATED CHARCOAL

PEBBLES

GLASS JAR

Nestle each carefully into its hole in the soil. Don't allow leaves to touch the sides—too much sun may burn leaves that are in direct contact with the container. Gently move soil around the roots and base of each plant. Be certain roots are not exposed.

STEP 7. If you'd like, add some pizzazz like moss, mini gnomes, dollhouse miniatures, shells, or driftwood around the plants.

STEP 8. Lightly water the terrarium. A spray bottle is great for this job.

STEP 9. Put a lid on it (unless it's going topless).

STEP 10. Place it by a window.

Terrarium Tips

Keep your plants happy. Check them periodically for pests and disease. Immediately remove weeds, dead foliage, and wilting plant parts. Many plants thrive in this stress-free environment and grow rather quickly. They may require regular pruning. Trim back towering plants so that shrimpy ones can get some sun. Also, remove and replace plumpish plants that take up too much elbow room.

OH, THE SCIENCE OF IT ALL!

How Does a Terrarium Work?

A terrarium is truly a small world—a tiny biosphere. It works like a scaled-down greenhouse. It's a closed ecological system, with a series of endless cycles.

- As plants photosynthesize and produce oxygen, they take up water through their roots and release it through their leaves (*transpiration*).
- When the warm water vapor leaves the plant (*evaporation*), it rises to the top of the terrarium (*convection*) and is trapped within the roof and walls.
- The water molecules accumulate and form droplets (*condensation*).
- The water droplets fall down the sides of the terrarium into the soil (*precipitation*).
- The water gathers in the soil until it evaporates or is taken up again by the plants.

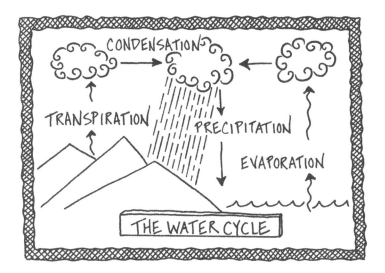

Top Terrarium Plants

Tuck a plant into anything cozy and sunny, and it will be a happy camper. Most mini shade-loving wildflowers, perennials, ground covers, mosses, ferns, grasses, orchids, bog plants, and carnivorous plants thrive in terrariums. You have lots of planting options. Take some risks. There are a few ground rules, though.

MAKE A LIST OF
POTENTIAL PLANTS
HERE

TOP TERRARIUM PLANTS

* Do some research. Head to your local nursery and determine which plant species would thrive in your terrarium.

* The best planting option is to adopt nursery-propagated mini native plants and nurture them under your wing, er, terrarium.

* Select plants that have similar environmental needs. Stick with either moisture-loving or heat-loving species. Don't mix the two, since they prefer different things.

* For minimal care, select species that won't outgrow the confines of the container. Choose plants that are petite and that will stay petite. Plants with one or more of the following in their scientific names are often good choices: *micro*, *minimus*, *minor*, *nanus*, *parcus*, *repens*, or *pumilus*. Or, if you're not picky, just plan to transplant things into roomier pots as they grow up.

EXPLORE MORE

There are many theories as to why being in nature makes us healthier. One leading hypothesis is that being outside increases vitamin D intake. Another hypothesis is that sunlight helps you sleep better. It sets the body's internal clock that tells you when to eat and sleep, and normalizes hormonal functions that occur at specific times of the day. Yet another hypothesis includes the idea that nature allows a clearer focused mind-set and a break from everyday stressors. In any case, it's clear that wonderful things happen when you head outside.

To become a modern pioneer, it's important to become reacquainted with the outside world. Get a dose of nature every day. Let a little sunshine into your life. In turn, you'll develop a lifelong passion for wild outdoor places. Here are more ways to get yourself out there.

PLAY IN THE SUN. Venture outside at least fifteen minutes every day. Recent studies reveal that most modern lifestyles prevent us from acquiring the levels of vitamin D that evolution intended us to have. Since dietary sources of vitamin D are minimal (found naturally in fish oils, fatty fish, and to a lesser extent in cheese, egg yolks, and certain mushrooms), the sun's UVB rays absorbed through the skin are our main source of this nutrient. Vitamin D protects against a host of diseases, including osteoporosis, heart disease, and cancers of the breast,

PLAY IN THE SUN

DATE	OUTSIDE ACTIVITY

prostate, and colon. Vitamin D has other hidden benefits—like protection from depression, insomnia, and an overactive immune system. Researchers cite decreased outdoor activity as one reason that people may become deficient in vitamin D, and state that far more lives are lost to diseases caused by lack of sunlight than to those caused by too much. Record your fifteen-minute vitamin D dosage on the handy chart on the previous page.

MAKE IT EASY TO GO OUTSIDE. Knowing something does not necessarily mean doing something. It can be a real challenge to get outside every day. Keep persevering. Outdoor time must be easy to do or it won't happen at all. Find storage bins or baskets to put near the front door and fill them with outdoor gear that will help you suit up and get out the door quickly: gloves, daypacks, mittens, scarves, hats, helmets, magnifying glasses, binoculars, field guides, compasses, notebooks, and pens. Start with short expeditions—a quick fifteen-minute jaunt is a massive accomplishment at the beginning—and then gradually soup them up and stretch them out. And when you're outside, think of more things to do. Involve other people. There's always an opportunity for everyone, even the tiniest or most sea-

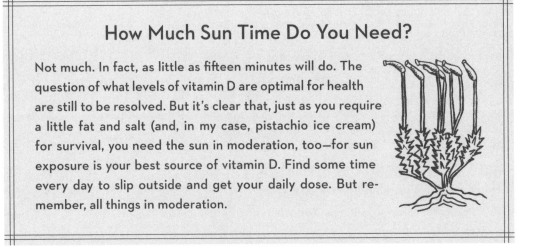

How Much Sun Time Do You Need?

Not much. In fact, as little as fifteen minutes will do. The question of what levels of vitamin D are optimal for health are still to be resolved. But it's clear that, just as you require a little fat and salt (and, in my case, pistachio ice cream) for survival, you need the sun in moderation, too—for sun exposure is your best source of vitamin D. Find some time every day to slip outside and get your daily dose. But remember, all things in moderation.

soned friend, to be included in the mix. Make your activities open-ended. Take your time. Leave room for exploration and discovery.

🌱 **FIND A REASON TO GO OUTSIDE EVERY DAY.** Even if you're familiar with all the whys and shoulds and you've got that burning, churning desire to get yourself out the door, there will certainly be days when your imagination runs completely dry. Don't scramble to come up with something fantastic to do. Have an arsenal of invincible ideas up your sleeve at all times.

The list of simple seasonal activities on the next page can serve as a catalyst for creative outdoor exploration. As the outside shifts from warm rain to dry heat and from icy rain to heavy snow, change your activities from sowing seeds to exploring the woods, and from planting bulbs to building snow forts. The seasons will guide you. Adapt the activities below to suit your particular climate. Prepare for the weather, or just prepare to get your feet wet. Or, try something listed in the summer during the winter— you'll be surprised how zippy you can feel racing bare- foot through fresh snow. Review the list and find something that speaks to you. Just get out there.

DOCUMENT IT

Get Outside

Making the initial decision to get outside on a regular basis is easy. Sticking with it, day after day, rain or shine, is the true challenge. To do it all year round, no matter what the weather is like, you should set up good habits immediately and stick with them. Write and sign a contract to take personal responsibility for your actions. The process of doing this can help you identify the obstacles that keep you from achieving your goal. Once you've identified these obstacles, you

SEASONAL THINGS TO GET YOU OUTSIDE

WINTER	SPRING
Search for animal tracks	Have an outdoor breakfast
Have a winter picnic	Hunt for signs of spring
Skip stones on an icy pond	Plant container herbs
Start a rock collection	Start a backyard garden
Build a snow fort	Make a nature hideout
Go sledding or skating	Visit a botanical garden
Hunt for bird and squirrel nests	Hang a birdhouse or birdfeeder
Look at ice through a magnifying glass	Go birdwatching
Start a winter nature journal	Hunt for spiderwebs
Identify backyard trees by bark	Clean up local trails
Melt a snowball	Hang a bird nesting ball
Whittle on your porch	Hunt for bugs
Examine snowflakes with a magnifying glass	Make a bee house
Hang and maintain a birdfeeder	Plant something—anything

SUMMER	FALL
Have a puddle-jumping contest	Fly a kite
Play kick the can or hide-and-seek	Go for a trail hike
Read aloud outside	Plant bulbs
Have an outdoor scavenger hunt	Collect leaves
Run barefoot through the grass	Build a fairy house
Follow an ant for 15 minutes	Build a fort
Camp out in the backyard	Run through a leaf pile
Make a backyard field guide	Plant a tree
Blow a grass whistle	Start a seed collection
Start a flower press	Winterize your garden
Explore under rocks and logs	Hang a bird or bat roosting box
Harvest something	Make a mudpie
Play in a puddle	Make bark rubbings
Go for a bike ride	Keep a moon diary
Count butterflies and moths	Sleep outside
Have a lemonade stand	Make a leaf press

ANYTIME	
Take a night hike	Climb a tree
Stargaze	Make a treasure map
Start a nature collection	Start a nature journal
Go cloud watching	Head out the door without a plan

can develop strategies to remove them from your path. Be specific and realistic. Take it seriously. Make a goal, and commit yourself to reach it despite all your excuses. Make things work out the way you want them to.

THE "GET OUTSIDE" CONTRACT

Goal:

I, _____ (your name here), hereby agree and commit to take the following steps to achieve my goal of _____

_____

(HINT: spending fifteen minutes outside every day).

The time I will spend outside will be dedicated to anything of my choosing.

I will start today.

In fact, I will start right now.

Potential Obstacles:

To avoid going outside, I am likely to use the following excuses:

_____

_____

Potential Excuse-Busters:

Instead of giving in to excuses, I plan to use the following counter-measures:

(e.g., find snorkeling gear, purchase racewalking shoes)

First, I will _____.

Then, I will _____.

Finally, I will _____.

I refuse to allow one small slipup to convince me that I've failed.

Signed, _____

Date: _____

—————————

Just beyond your doorstep is a sun-filled world waiting to be explored—a flourishing forest, a roadside field, an abandoned lot, a sidewalk crack. No matter where you live, the wild world is at your fingertips. No exotic setting, no special equipment required. All you need is a desire to open your door and let a little sunshine into your life. Get outside and play in the sun. It's good for you. It should be something you practice every single day.

4

Spend Time Wisely

How we spend our days is, of course,
how we spend our lives.
—ANNIE DILLARD

Not so very long ago, humans moved through the world at a measured pace—marking time by the sun's overhead passing and the seasons' annual rhythms. The day began and ended with the sun—we woke and fed the kettle's fire, prepared meals, mended torn clothing, felled trees, chopped wood, and fetched water. We spent time trapping, planting, harvesting, preparing, cooking, and storing food. The day ended at nightfall when the animals were cooped and stabled. There was no precise separation between work and play—weeks were infused with neighborhood apple-paring, barn-raising, and cheese-making parties. There were quilting bees and spelling bees in town when we walked there. Things like churning butter and taking a bath were big undertakings. It took more time to get things done. Because of this, we were immersed in the present. We stayed in the same spot for a while.

We watched time pass. Resting was not considered *inaction*. It was considered *relaxation*.

Things have recently gotten complicated. And they are getting progressively more so. Today, we're multitaskers hastily ordering tall half skinny, half 1 percent extra-hot café mochas, whipped cream, and no sugar. *Pronto!*

These days, just about everything we do depends in some way on getting somewhere on time, meeting someone quickly, and leaving punctually. Most people operate within a margin of plus or minus a few minutes. Some people, mostly astronomers, particle physicists, and 100-meter butterfly Olympic swimmers, measure time in seconds and fractions of a second. There is continual pressure to fine-tune our timing. As we're faced with a near-constant stream of stimuli and appointments, slowing down is a conscious choice.

Faster is not always better. As we're rushing to keep up, we're falling further behind. We're not letting things sink in. We're holding our breath rather than breathing. We're disconnected from nature and its careful pace, and are completely out of sync with our deepest selves.

Modern pioneers know the extraordinary thing that happens when you become still in nature: you become familiar with the stillness and silence at the center of all the buzz. And it's there, you know. It's at the heart of everything. There is a quiet sanctuary in nature where you can find respite from it all.

In this chapter, you'll practice being present. You'll take your time. You'll rest your brain and slow down enough to feel yourself alive. Time is arguably our most valuable commodity: spend it wisely; it slips by whether or not you opt to cram it full of meaning. Cherish the present—make the most of every sunrise. Feel the moment of now. Break things into tiny manageable bits. Think about what each bite-size piece is made of, and what each has to offer. Consider every morsel—every ordinary ritual of life. This is how things happen—step by step, dish by dish, sip by sip, and word by word. Be here. Right now. In real time.

Tree Stump Sundial

A sundial was one of the first tools used to measure the flow of time. Given a few basic supplies, you can whip up this practical timekeeping device—the most ancient of scientific instruments—based on reliable natural cycles around you. Easy to set up and read, a handmade equatorial sundial displays time from sunrise to sunset. Use this simple tool to get some insight into the nature of your world, and to remind you to spend your time more wisely.

PROJECT STEPS

STEP 1. Get your hands on a sliced tree stump. Circumference size does not matter, though the slice should be very flat and no thicker than 3 centimeters. This will act as the *base plate* of your sundial and will represent the plane of the Earth's equator.

STEP 2. Determine the center of the base plate's front. To do this, use a pencil and ruler to draw a line (a *chord*) across the base, closer to one side so it cuts the base into two unequal semicircles. Make the line's length a nice even number—10, 20, or 26 centimeters. Measure exactly halfway along the line, and use a protractor to draw a line perpendicular to the chord all the way to the other side of the base. Repeat to draw another chord and

TREE STUMP SUNDIAL MATERIALS
- SLICED TREE STUMP
- PROTRACTOR
- SCISSORS
- RULER
- PENCIL
- SANDPAPER
- MASKING TAPE
- UTILITY KNIFE
- PERMANENT MARKER
- ¼ INCH WOOD DOWEL
- DRILL AND ¼ INCH BIT
- WOOD GLUE
- CONSTRUCTION PAPER
- BUBBLE LEVEL
- WIDE CHISEL ⎤
- WOODEN MALLET ⎟ OPTIONAL
- FANCY NUMBERS ⎦

Before You Start

Your sundial will be positioned according to where you find yourself in the world. The instructions for this project apply to the Western Hemisphere, north of the equator. If you live in Swaziland or New Zealand, you'll have to do some tweaking. No matter where you live, the angle of your sundial will be dependent upon your latitude on Earth. This measurement makes up for the tilt of the Earth and will determine the angle of your sundial. Before you start, consult an atlas to determine where on the world you are.

KEEP TRACK OF YOUR LATITUDE COORDINATES RIGHT HERE:
_____

perpendicular line. Draw as many chords and perpendicular lines as you like. The point where all perpendicular lines meet is the center of the base. Mark it with a pencil.

STEP 3. With a ¼-inch bit, drill a hole in the center of the base, all the way through to the other side.

STEP 4. Use sandpaper to smooth the rough edges of the base on both sides. Sand away all pencil markings.

STEP 5. With a ruler and pencil, draw a line from one edge of the base to the other, passing directly through the drilled center hole. Mark a point on the exact bottom and top of the base. The *bottom* of the base will be 12:00 p.m.

STEP 6. Turn the base over. Mark the exact bottom of the base, matching the 12:00 p.m. mark on the base's front.

Selecting a Sundial Base

It's important to keep in mind that a sundial base (or *dial plate*) can be made from an almost infinite variety of materials. A sliced tree stump is a nice choice, but really anything round and disc-like will do for this project. Pie plate, wooden disk, old record—they are all fine alternatives, just maybe not as permanent. Keep in mind that you must somehow make a ¼-inch hole in the center. To make it easy, I'll assume that you plan to use a tree stump.

STEP 7. Cut out the sundial templates below and glue them onto two separate pieces of construction paper. With a pencil and ruler, extend the template lines onto the construction paper.

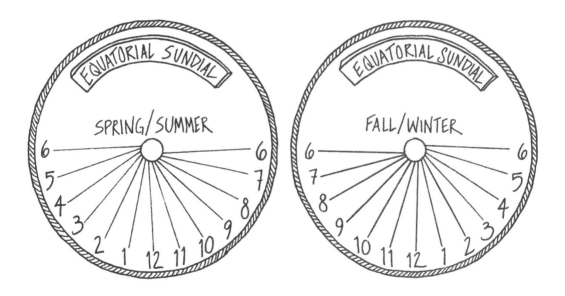

STEP 8. Poke a hole through the center of each template with a pencil. Place the Spring/Summer template over the base, matching center holes and time marks. Roughly cut the paper template the size of the

base. Tape the paper's sides to the base with masking tape to ensure that it stays in place. Use a ruler and utility knife to carefully score several reference points along each line onto the underlying wood. Remove the paper template. With ruler and pencil, join the reference points together to mark out each line on the dial. These lines will mark each hour on the sundial.

STEP 9. Using a permanent marker, mark the lines on the dial. Or, if you have extra time on your hands, use a wide chisel and wooden mallet to create fixed shallow grooves along the lines.

STEP 10. Using a permanent marker, label the lines with corresponding numbers. As a fancy alternative, use dice, domino pieces, or small wood-burned or metal-stamped numbers to mark the dial. Adhere with wood glue.

STEP 11. Repeat Steps 8, 9, and 10 for the base plate's other side, using the Fall/Winter Dial Plate Template.

STEP 12. Place the sundial on a table with the Spring/Summer side facing up. Push a wood dowel through the center of the base. Since it will represent the Earth's spin axis, the dowel should be perfectly perpendicular to the base. Continue to push

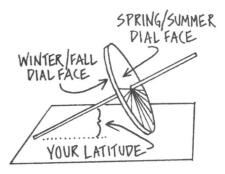

it through the base's center until the angle between the dowel and the table is the same exact measurement as your latitude (e.g., if you live at 43 degrees longitude, the sundial's angle should be set at 43 degrees). Use a protractor to check your accuracy. Glue the dowel in place and allow it to dry overnight.

STEP 13. At exactly noon on a sunny day, find a spot that will be in sunlight for a full day. Use a bubble level to ensure that the surface is horizontal. To determine true north—the geographic North Pole where all longitude lines meet—position the sundial on the flat surface with the Spring/Summer side facing up. Place it perfectly level. Orient the dial so that the dowel casts a shadow directly over the 12:00 hour line. To accurately display time, your sundial must always face this direction. Depending on the season, the shadow will be cast on either the Spring/Summer side or the Fall/Winter side of the sundial. (Tip: Don't use a compass to find north—a compass shows magnetic north, not true north.)

STEP 14. As time passes and the dowel's shadow moves away from noon, cut the dowel on the sundial's Spring/Summer side to size, leaving just enough dowel length to cast a shadow over the farthest numbers early or late in the day.

OH, THE SCIENCE OF IT ALL!

How Does a Sundial Work?

A sundial is in essence simply any form of stick, known as a *gnomon* (pronounced "NO-men"), that casts a shadow on a base, known as the *dial plate*, when the sun shines on it. The shadow's position is used to indicate the passage of time. The Earth rotates on its axis about once every 24 hours, traveling 15 degrees every hour, and the Earth revolves around the sun once a year. As the earth rotates and the sun appears to move across the sky, the shadow of the gnomon's edge progressively aligns with different hour lines on the sundial's base. As the Earth rotates eastward, the gnomon's shadow progresses from hour to hour.

The sundial is actually a reduced model of the Earth. The sundial's base is aligned with the celestial equator. During the summer months, the Earth is tilted toward the sun. The shadow of the sundial's gnomon will be cast on the sundial's front face. During the cooler months, when the sun is low on the horizon, the shadow of the gnomon will be cast on the sundial's back face.

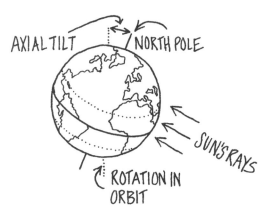

When you look at the sun, you see it from an eternally moving platform. As you (standing on Earth) rotate eastward and the sun moves across the sky, each 15-degree Earth rotation is equivalent to 1 hour. The sun's apparent motion across the celestial sphere in the course of a year is not perfect, though. It's a little wonky. This is caused by two factors. First, the Earth's orbit is not circular; it is elliptical, with the sun being closer to one end. Second, the Earth is tilted with respect to the plane of its orbit by about

23.5 degrees. In the Northern Hemisphere, this inclination causes the sun to appear at its highest point in the sky in June and its lowest point in December. It's the fusion of these things that's responsible for seasonal change and daily variations in time. Days are not constant. A sundial measures *solar time*, which varies a bit during the year because of the Earth's wonky motion.

To average out the above differences and give us an exact 24-hour day, your electric alarm clock keeps constant seconds and uses *standard mean time* based on an imaginary Earth moving at constant speed in a perfectly circular orbit with its rotational axis perpendicular to its orbital plane. The difference between these two time measurements is known as the *equation of time*. A graph of the equation of time, determined either through mathematical calculation or direct observation, looks something like this:

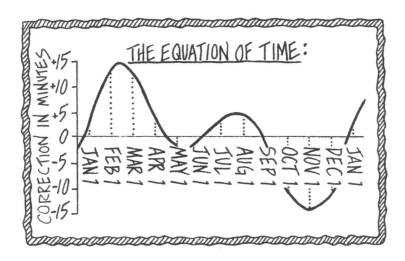

Tell Sundial Time

To read time accurately, a sundial must face true north in a sunny spot. Place your sundial in this position (see Step 13). Notice that its hour-lines radiate tangentially from the center of the gnomon and are spaced exactly 15 degrees apart from one another. The gnomon's shadow falls in the opposite direction of the sun. Because the Earth rotates counterclockwise (as viewed from above the Northern Hemisphere), the gnomon's shadow moves in a clockwise direction. Therefore, morning times are located on the right side of the Spring/Summer dial face, and afternoon times are on the left.

To tell time, look closely at the gnomon's shadow. One edge of the shadow, called the *style*, will be used as the time-telling edge. From spring equinox (around March 20 in the Northern Hemisphere) to fall equinox (around September 22 in the Northern Hemisphere), the gnomon will cast a shadow on the Spring/Summer dial face. After fall equinox, the gnomon will cast a shadow on the Fall/Winter dial face. For even greater time-telling precision, locate the current date on the "Equation of Time" graph and add or subtract the number of minutes indicated.

EXPLORE MORE

In today's fast-paced world, often the ultimate challenge is to just be present. To notice what's right in front of you. To live in the moment. To harness your concentration and let go of time—of schedules and constraints. Imagine yourself incapable of seeing your past or your future. Pretend you just got here. Forget yesterday. Forget today. In the present, everything is new. Here are a few more ways to slow down and feel the moment of now.

🌱 **BE PRESENT.** Sit down for 10 minutes every single day. For one week, record direct observations about the natural world around you—what you see, what you smell, what you hear. No metaphors, no interpretations, no comparisons, no abstractions, just reality. Let things be things. Look straight into the world's eyes—the bird perched on a wire, the orange slice, the floating seed. Here they are. Right here.

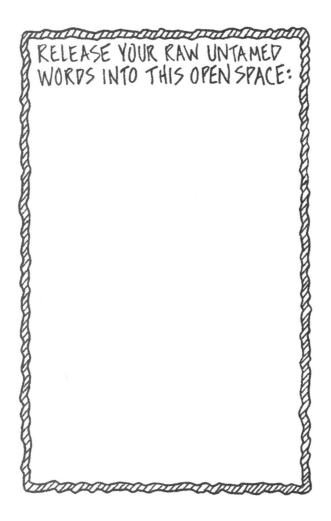

RELEASE YOUR RAW UNTAMED WORDS INTO THIS OPEN SPACE:

SLICE UP YOUR DAY. Don't get stuck with too much on your plate. Get some portion control. Certainly there are things you want to spend more time doing—like stargazing, writing limericks, playing the thumb piano, and whittling. Make time for them. Reclaim your spare moments—even if they're few and far between.

Make a pie chart of all the things you'd like to fit into your day. Assign sizable slices to things you love. Build time into your day to do the big slices. Schedule them in. Consider what your day has to offer. There's always room for the good stuff.

PLAN TO HAVE NO PLAN. Never underestimate the value of doing nothing. Find some time to head out the door with no plan whatsoever. As your day unfolds, allow yourself to be lost in the slowness of the moment. Let go of doing something specific and be prepared for spontaneous activities that spring up. Spend time in a useless manner. It's good for you.

JUMP INTO YOUR STREAM. The downside of RSS feeds and chat-streams and social networking timelines and everyday chaos is that you may not actually know what's happening inside your own stream. You have a lot to think about.

Choose a broad topic, find a comfy spot, and start writing. Forget grammar, sentence structure, and staying on topic. Write backwards, upside down, or in a trapezoidal shape. Write in a meandering spiral starting from the page's center, or in a starburst of phrases. Harvest your thoughts, chop them up, pour them onto the page, and make a thick simmering stew of ideas. Keep writing until you run out of words.

IN THIS SPACE, WRITE YOUR STREAM OF CONSCIOUSNESS —
WHATEVER POPS INTO YOUR HEAD.

DOCUMENT IT

Slow Way Down

Find alternatives to cramming your days full. Check off this list of ways to slow yourself down.

The Slow Way Down Checklist

❑ Reconnect with your natural body. Any practice that brings your attention back to yourself—yoga, drum circle, African dance—can help reduce stress and anxiety.

- ❑ Disconnect with screens. Close your laptop, turn off your phone and TV, and lose the watch. Be more real-world social. Laugh with someone. Shake hands. Give real hugs.

- ❑ Play with people and pets—tell stories, get together, and surround yourself with the very young, the very old, and the very furry. They know how to spend a good day.

- ❑ Don't multitask. Make a connection with the things you do, rather than just ticking them off a to-do list (like this one—aaack!). Take your time.

- ❑ Get outside. Take a long walk on a remote trail or beach, sit near a stream, and lie under the clouds.

- ❑ Breathe. Pause. Take a breath. Take a morning nap, read poetry, or indulge in an evening bubble bath.

- ❑ Live in slow motion. Double the time you think it should take you to complete a task. This doesn't mean being lazy; it just means living your life at the right speed, not at a frenzied pace.

- ❑ Grow and harvest something. A simple pot of herbs on a windowsill is perfect. Protect it. Take care of it. Watch it grow. Harvest it.

- ❑ Be mindful and present. Sit still. Settle in. Take the time to learn a place's secrets.

- ❑ Just say no. Do less stuff. And, if you do sign up, ask for help.

———————

An amazing thing happens when you slow down. You become so accustomed to living in the "now" that each moment of your day seems like a gift. You take advantage of every sunrise and sunset. You focus on the feeling of your body breathing, your mind thinking, and the dynamic space around you—filled with living and growing wild things—stirring and shifting. You give the world your complete attention. You recognize that these things are there and you are living within them and absorbing them, and that you can stay in one place and still quietly grow.

5

Get Dirty

In the spring, at the end of the day,
you should smell like dirt.
—MARGARET ATWOOD

If you are an epidemiologist, an infectious disease specialist, a nursery school teacher, or a long-distance swimmer who has tackled the length of the Mississippi River, then you are more than familiar with a weekend of misfortune and bed rest that can come from an array of pathogens. Viruses, bacteria, fungi, and protozoa—all are infectious agents that can disrupt the normal physiology of a host animal or plant and wreak complete havoc. It's a germy world out there.

Pathogens are everywhere. In fact, many yucky hot spots are in places you'd consider clean. The kitchen sink and sponge, the toothbrush holder, the pet bowl, the stove knobs—all are five-star germ hotels. Chilling headlines of tuberculosis, food poisoning, cholera, and meningitis have led to an outright war on an invisible enemy, fought with antibacterial soap, antimicrobial cleanser, and antifungal cream. Rarely do you hear a parent say, "Make sure you get yourself good and filthy!"

Overall, when it comes to germs, though, most folks actually have it backward. With relatively few exceptions, germs are good for us. I admit, there are a few bacteria I'd rather not meet, but the majority of them are completely harmless, and many are highly beneficial. Your body houses millions of microorganisms on the skin and within the nose, mouth, and gut—even your eyelashes most likely house tiny arthropods called *Demodex* mites. Each spot on and within your body hosts a radically different cast of characters. In fact, up to 90 percent of your cells are actually not *yours*—instead they are living (and dying) microbes. Without them you wouldn't survive. They help you digest your food, produce life-sustaining nutrients, and occupy tiny niches that would otherwise be inhabited by petulant pathogens.

Think of yourself as more than a single organism. Your body is a planet—a superorganism comprised of so much more than your own human cells. Its sun-drenched skin grasslands and waterlogged gut wetlands are teeming with diverse communities of critters—each looking for a shelter, a good meal, and a few trustworthy allies.

It's true—bacteria cause disease. The idea that they might also prevent disease seems counterintuitive. Keeping your environment clean is smart, but the path we're heading down lately is actually destroying the microbes that help strengthen our immune systems and maintain an ecological balance. Exposure to germs has been proven to defend against allergies and asthma, and to increase serotonin production. In fact, kids who are raised in "germy" environments like farms or pet-filled homes are much less likely to develop allergies, eczema, or autoimmune diseases, suggesting they have stronger immune systems than kids raised in ultraclean environments. Our teeny-weeny sidekicks perform critical lifesaving tasks for us—swiftly attacking bad guys and keeping everything in check.

Are we too clean? Clearly, living with microbes demands a biological balancing act. Dirtiness comes with a price. But, cleanliness comes with a price, too. Certainly, I don't propose a return to the pre-antibiotic germ-filled environment of yesteryear, but I do advocate a restoration of equilibrium.

In this chapter, you'll expose yourself to the germy world. You'll be challenged to go barefoot in the dirt, make a mudpie, snuggle with a dog, and eat whole unprocessed fiber-rich antibiotic-free foods that promote a healthy internal ecosystem—feed your microbuddies the foods they fancy. You'll be advised to wash your hands with plain soap and water after painting your porch, but not after planting petunias. You'll be urged to go outside and get yourself good and dirty and restore the ecosystems of your own body planet.

✦ TRY THIS ✦

Cackleberry Sprouts

If you were a Southern poultry farmer, you'd wake up and carefully collect a dozen warm cackleberries—Mmmm! Fresh eggs!—from your henhouse each morning. Then, you would bake two jumbo pound cakes and serve them lightly toasted with whipped cream and raspberry preserves. As a result, you'd have a dozen eggshells on your hands looking for a job. This project below would be perfect for you. If you were *you*, though, and you washed your hands any time within the past few days, this would also be the perfect project for you, since it would help get you good and grimy.

Grab a dozen eggs and grow some cackleberry sprouts. Expose yourself to the jumble of sand, silt, clay, microorganisms, and decomposing organic matter we call soil. Get up close and personal. Get some dirt under your fingernails, into your pockets, and deep into your nooks and crannies. Dig in!

CACKLEBERRY SPROUT MATERIALS
- 1 DOZEN EGGSHELLS
- 1 EGG CARTON
- SEEDS
- SEED STARTING MIX
- SCISSORS
- SEWING NEEDLE
- SHARP KNIFE
- LARGE PLASTIC CONTAINER
- WATER

PROJECT STEPS

STEP 1. Bring all the project materials someplace where you can comfortably make a big mess.

STEP 2. Remove the egg carton's top with scissors.

STEP 3. Carefully prick a tiny drainage hole in the bottom of each shell with a sewing needle. To remove the egg contents, create a small opening in the top of each shell—about the size of a dime—with a sharp knife.

STEP 4. Pour out the contents—if this is tricky, scramble the eggs inside the shell with a toothpick and then pour them out. Gently pinch each eggshell open until a third of each shell is removed. Wash each empty eggshell thoroughly and place it back in the egg carton.

STEP 5. Fill each eggshell with moist seed-starting mix to 1 to 2 centimeters below the shell opening. Place the soil-filled shells into the egg carton.

STEP 6. Select some seeds. Really, any will do. I'm partial to beans, basil, zinnias, sunflowers, and fancy purplish flowers.

STEP 7. Using a finger, poke a small indentation in the center of the soil. Follow the instructions on the seed packet for proper planting depth. The general rule is to plant three times deeper than the size of the seed.

STEP 8. Place a seed or two into each hole and lightly cover the seed with soil.

STEP 9. Use a permanent marker to label each eggshell with seed type.

STEP 10. Moisten the soil again gently with a few drops of water. Allow the water to saturate the soil, but be careful not to drown the seeds.

STEP 11. Seed germination is highly dependent on water. So, to help retain necessary moisture, cover the egg carton lightly with a large transparent plastic container. Find a good spot for them. Generally a warm windowsill is best. Monitor your seedlings daily. They should be kept evenly moist, but not saturated. You should begin to see sprouts in ten to fourteen days, depending on seed type.

STEP 12. A few weeks after germination, your eggshells will house a flock of able-bodied, rosy-cheeked seedlings. Remove the transparent plastic container. Keep the seedlings inside until they have three to four *true leaves* (rows of leaves above the first pair of leaves).

STEP 13. Before moving your cackleberry sprouts outside, take a few weeks to gradually introduce them to their new growing conditions. This "hardening off" gives the seedlings a chance to acclimate to sunlight, drying winds, and climate changes. On warm days, move the seedlings outside to a shady spot for increasing amounts of time, several days in a row. If the temperature looks like it will drop, bring them back inside. Progressively increase the amount of time and sunlight they receive outside until they appear ready to venture out on their own.

STEP 14. On a mild cloudy day, plant the seedlings directly in the ground, carefully crushing the bottom part of the eggshell so the roots can emerge. Water the transplants gently, but thoroughly.

What Do Eggshells Bring to the Party?

Calcium is the bedrock of healthy organic soil—it maintains the chemical balance in dirt, reduces salinity, and improves water penetration. It's an essential nutrient for plant growth—used in the formation of wood and in the maintenance of cell walls within plant tissue. The simple act of adding eggshells improves soil structure and helps plants get the nutrients they need, in a form they can use, when they need it.

OH, THE SCIENCE OF IT ALL!

Can Dirt Make You Smarter?

Getting dirty is good stuff. And luckily, research reveals that a strain of soil bacteria (*Mycobacterium vaccae*) can be just what the doctor ordered. Exposure to this particular bacterium not only lowers depression and anxiety, but also makes you smarter. Mice fed tiny *M. vaccae* sandwiches (yum!) are able to navigate tricky mazes twice as fast as mice fed a normal mouse diet. And they are less anxious. The body's immune response to *M. vaccae* triggers the brain to release serotonin, a neurotransmitter (a chemical messenger between nerve cells) and mood-regulating chemical. It's thought to play a role in learning. Lack of serotonin is one symptom, or perhaps even the cause, of depression.

What does this research mean? It means that gardeners inhale these bacteria while digging in the soil, and also encounter them in freshly harvested vegetables. It means that this tiny bacterium can benefit us through normal everyday soil contact. It means that outdoor learning environments—like school and community gardens—may decrease anxiety and improve the ability to learn new things. It means it's good to get yourself good and dirty.

~ PROOF OF DIRTY YOU ~

PROVE THAT YOU'VE GOTTEN DIRTY.
PLACE YOUR GRUBBY FINGERPRINTS RIGHT HERE.

Turn Some Stones

A mere handful of forest soil is home to more microorganisms than there are people on Earth—thousands of bacterial species, hundreds of fungal and protozoan species, dozens of nematode species, and a hodgepodge of mites, micro-arthropods, earthworms, insects, mini vertebrates, and plants.

Tiny one-celled bacteria, algae, fungi, and protozoa are visible only with the help of a microscope, but larger, more complex arthropods, earthworms, slugs, fungi, and insects are discernible to any inspired explorer willing to overturn and then delicately replace a few medium-sized rocks or logs. Go out and hunt for a spot with a good collection of homes—a morning following a good rain is perfect timing—and carefully look underneath.

This is like the ultimate surprise party—you never know who will be hiding behind something and then jump out. Surprise! Be prepared for any type of guest—field cricket, millipede, grub, pillbug, or salamander. Remember, you're opening the door to someone else's home, so replace their roof delicately and in the same exact position it was when you happened upon it. And, of course, thank everybody for having you over.

EXPLORE MORE

Research shows that people exposed to soil microbes and bacteria develop superior immune systems and increased levels of serotonin—clearly dirt can make us both happy and healthy. One of the best ways you can get

DIY Magnifying Glass

If you're bent on getting an even closer look at something or somebody but you find yourself without a magnifying glass, just make your own! Grab a smooth, clear plastic bottle from the recycling bin, a permanent marker, and scissors. Draw and cut out a 10-centimeter circle near the neck of the bottle. Pour water into the disk. Hold the disk over the object you'd like to view more closely.

CUT AND FILL WITH WATER

How does this work? Sunlight passes through the water and is refracted—it is bent inward—creating a lens effect. Remember: a lens concentrates the sun's rays onto one small area. If left in the same spot, the magnifying glass can rapidly heat things up. Be careful!

dirty is to get outside and make your very own soil. Many people start doing this for practical reasons—composting garden waste and food scraps in an effort to reduce unnecessary household garbage. But there are other reasons why you should consider diverting your organic waste away from a landfill. As much as 30 percent of your garbage is a nutrient-rich resource for soil microorganisms and can improve soil structure, maintain moisture levels, and keep everything in check underground. If you start to consider your organic waste as a potential resource for the complex web of your backyard critters, you'll find yourself addressing real-world issues by restoring the ecological health of your own backyard.

Your kitchen spews out a steady supply of compostable riches. Incorporate nature's organic recycling plan into every day. With or without a compost pile, you can reduce your trash and improve the soil. Composting requires very little effort or resources, and it has a huge positive impact on the environment. There's no "right way" to compost—just choose whichever method matches your space and dedication level. Here are a few ways to get out there and get dirty:

Method 1. Toss Small Scraps. You don't need a compost bin to make compost. Some things—tea leaves, used coffee grounds, chopped banana peels, and crushed eggshells—can be tossed directly into the garden. Sprinkle these kitchen scraps around the base of your plants to give your plants an almost immediate nitrogen, calcium, potassium, and magnesium boost. Don't add too much at once, and don't add more scraps until the original scraps decompose.

Method 2. Try Trench Composting. If you don't want the hassle of maintaining a compost bin, but you dream of enriching your garden's soil, trench composting may be the ideal solution. In an unused garden bed, dig a hole about 30 centimeters deep, put 7 to 10 centimeters of chopped kitchen scraps into the pit, cover the scraps with a thin layer of dry brown leaves, and top with at least 15 centimeters of soil. As the organic matter in the trench decomposes, nutrients become available for nearby plants. This anaerobic method takes longer than aerobic bin composting—it could take up to a year—but is perfect if you don't have a compost bin.

Method 3. Compost in a Bin or Heap. If you have some elbow room, take it a step further and start a proper compost pile. Just heap the stuff together in a backyard corner until the pile is big enough to merit some attention. Then every so often, when you're in a composting sort of mood, grab your pitchfork and mix the pile up, adding water to make it a little

COMPOSTABLE THINGS

Do Compost	Do Not Compost
Vegetable scraps	Plastics
Grains and pasta	Animal products
Fruit rinds and peels	Oily foods
Breads and cereals	Dairy products
Coffee grounds and filters	Your piano music that you can't figure out
Tea bags	
Eggshells	Diseased plants
Dryer lint	Heavily coated or glossy paper
Grass clippings	Nonbiodegrable materials
Bark, leaves, and twigs	Toxic materials
Pine needles	Invasive plants
Dead plants	Waste from carnivorous pets

moist. Add a variety of scraps to the pile. Compost happens thanks to the efforts of a vast population of organisms. Each organic ingredient you discard—parsnip peeling, squash stalk, or turnip top—hosts a slightly different group of helpful critters. Diversity makes compost greater than the sum of its parts. To speed up the process, you can pay attention to ratios of browns (things that are slow to rot) and greens (things that are quick to rot), layer things in a tumbler or circular wire fencing, record heap temperature, and use a compost sifter. Get as fancy as you'd like. Rest assured, any way you do it, you'll eventually have earthy nutrient-rich compost on your hands.

COMPOST LAYERS

GRASS CLIPPINGS
SOIL
DRY LEAVES
KITCHEN SCRAPS
TWIGS AND BRANCHES

Growing Soil

The Earth itself is something of a compost pile. Compost happens thanks to the efforts of a multitude of organisms—from worms to pillbugs to teeny fungi and bacteria—that convert organic matter into great stuff plants can easily use. Soil formation is a remarkably slow process—accumulation of just a few centimeters of healthy soil can take five hundred to a thousand years! Composting is little more than speeding up and intensifying natural processes.

DOCUMENT IT

Get Dirty

Get dirty as much as possible. Add to this messy to-do list and check things off as you go.

The Get Dirty Checklist

- ❏ Walk outside barefoot.

- ❏ Roll down a grassy hill.

- ❏ Make the messiest mudpie ever.

- ❏ Mix up some seedbombs.

- ❏ Make a muddy river and jump in.

- ❏ Plant something. Anything.

- ❏ Harvest something edible. Eat it.

- ❏ Catch a tadpole.

- ❏ Hunt for critters under rocks.

- ❏ Start a compost pile.

- ❏ Make a windowsill herb garden.

- ❏ Go on an outdoor scavenger hunt.

- ❏ Crawl around and pretend you're a bug.

- ❏ Play wild hide-and-seek.

- ❏ Dig for buried treasure.

- ❏ Lie on the grass.

- ❏ Find a Y-shaped twig.

- ❏ Collect pebbles that look like toes.

- ❏ Pretend you're asleep while lying on the grass.

- ❏ Really fall asleep while pretending to be asleep while lying on the grass.

- ❏ _____

- ❏ _____

A little dirt never hurt. In fact, exposure to its germs has been shown to be highly beneficial. A modern pioneer recognizes this and knows the word "human" originates from the same root as the root "humus," a component of soil. A modern pioneer considers the Earth itself as something of a compost pile and understands that essentially all life is dependent on the establishment of a healthy nutrient-rich foundation of soil. Now is your big chance. Get out there and play in the dirt.

6

See the Big Picture

As the crickets' soft autumn hum is to us, so are we to
the trees, as are they to the rocks and the hills.
—GARY SNYDER

The Earth is chock-full
of highly organized structures
that have somehow evolved from the simple
rules of physics. Our world unfolds in dynamic
patterns of change—solar and lunar cycles, seasonal weather,
plant and animal growth—providing opportunity for constant
transformation, fluctuation, and renewal. Each season has its
own character—a chorus of spring peepers, sweet summer wildflower per-
fume, and long, cool winter shadows. As well, there is continual metamorphosis of tremendous landforms and ecosystems—generally indiscernible,
and every so often at breakneck speed. Around us, critters can tune in to

their surroundings and change accordingly—shed skin, disperse seeds, or cache extra nuts for tricky times.

Resiliency is part of nature. Many critters including microbes, fish, amphibians, and mammals are undaunted when they're put in a jam. If you're a male clownfish living in a secluded venomous sea anemone near Papua New Guinea and your sole companion is another male clownfish, you may be forced to slowly transform your body into that of a female for the sake of gene survival. In fact, you and your partner may live happily ever after—prudently picking phytoplankton and zooplankton off your quaint anemone home and making a lifetime of peppy clownfish babies. If you're a marine microbe trapped in Antarctic ice for one hundred thousand years and have just been brought by a microbiologist into a cozy New Jersey laboratory, it's likely you can be completely revived and lead a full life of active bacteria metabolization—doubling in colony size every few months or so. If you're a tiny seed living in dim tropical rainforest understory soil and your neighboring Brazil nut tree has fallen in a storm, you seize the chance to sneak through the canopy gap. *Carpe diem!*

There is constant rebirth and cyclic change in nature. When's the next full moon? When's raspberry season? When's spring hawk migration? Milestones like these are happening all around you all the time, but chances are you've overlooked them. Not so long ago, watching natural cycles was serious business. Early pioneers sowed and harvested crops, pruned trees, slaughtered farm animals, and cut firewood based on the lunar phases. Everyone was familiar with seasonally shifting asterisms and constellations in the night sky—the result of our planet's changing orientation relative to the sun.

Shift your focus. Become reacquainted with the natural rhythms around you. You'll look at the world differently. You'll see patterns all around you, you'll recognize the fundamental interdependence of it all, and you'll see yourself embedded within, and ultimately dependent upon, nature's cycles. You'll see that you, too, are not a fixed and finished object. You're a lifelong learner who creatively adapts to your changing circumstances. And you'll treat the Earth really well—the way you'd treat a dear old friend.

✦ TRY THIS ✦

Ecological Calendar

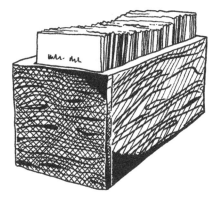

Our world is not static—it is transient and continually changing. Nature skillfully organizes and reinvents itself within this eternal metamorphosis. You can see this in repetitive patterns like the Earth's seasons, the tidal cycle, and the stages of plant growth and reproduction. As well, there are huge changes we seldom see—things that may happen over the course of many thousands of years like landform and ecosystem transformation and the irreversible trajectory of species evolution. We are in a world of replicating patterns with organisms responding differently to change over time. A garden snail is not exactly as it was thousands of years ago. And *we* are not the same.

Notice the changes around you and create a handmade perpetual calendar to keep a record of them. Keep everything in one spot—a daily reminder of important things and the rhythms around you. Compare events year after year and recognize cyclical patterns and unforeseen anomalies. Forecast approaching events and prepare for them ahead of time. Timing in life is everything!

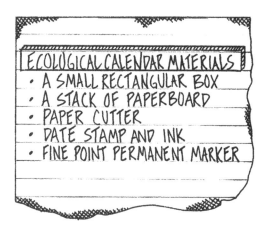

ECOLOGICAL CALENDAR MATERIALS
- A SMALL RECTANGULAR BOX
- A STACK OF PAPERBOARD
- PAPER CUTTER
- DATE STAMP AND INK
- FINE POINT PERMANENT MARKER

PROJECT STEPS

STEP 1. Collect a stack of paperboard from the recycling bin (good candidates are greeting cards, postcards, thick cardstock, and dry grocery boxes). You'll need more than you think. Stash your stack in a special spot.

STEP 2. Measure the inside box dimensions to determine the card size. Trim the stack of cards to fit perfectly inside the box, but measuring 1 centimeter taller than the box. Cut a few extra cards the same width, but 2 centimeters taller. These will act as dividers. You'll need 366 separate cards (the extra one is for February 29), plus a few additional dividers.

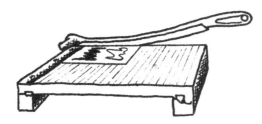

STEP 3. Stamp the back of each card with the month and day up top. Omit the year, since you'll use the calendar from year to year. Leave the dividers unstamped, or label them with months, special occasions, or photos.

STEP 4. Stack the cards in the box by date with the current date in the front. Use the dividers to feature specific months or days. Each day, place the prior day's card in the back of the deck.

STEP 5. Store your perpetual calendar in a handy spot with a pen alongside it. Chronicle seasonal events, daily sightings, important milestones, and annual happenings around you. Jot down a brief word or two each week, or keep a meticulous record of daily experiences—it's up to you!

Choosing a Box

Most likely your closet, local thrift store, or flea market has a funky box that will fit the cards you have in mind. A metal tin, old recipe box, or long wooden crate would be perfect for the job. Keep in mind that the box's length will depend on the thickness of the date cards you plan to use. Thin cardstock may only fill up a tin recipe box, but thick paperboard may require a long lanky wooden drawer. No lid required—going topless is actually better. Pick a seasoned box that has led a full life, but needs a little pick-me-up.

OH, THE SCIENCE OF IT ALL!

What Causes Seasons?

The Earth orbits the sun elliptically and, at the same time, spins on an axis that is tilted relative to its plane of orbit. Seasons are caused by this tilt away or toward the sun as the Earth travels through its year-long path around the sun. In the Northern Hemisphere (above the equator), the tilt toward the sun is maximized in late June (summer solstice). In late December (winter solstice), the Earth's tilt away from the sun is maximized. The seasons are reversed in the Southern Hemisphere. From year to year, there is always variability in equinoxes and solstices because of the way the Earth's changing tilt matches up with its orbit around the sun.

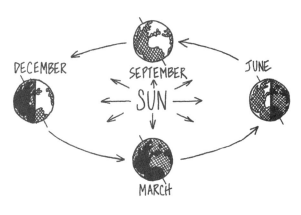

Tune in and Take Notes

Recognize that your landscape depends on something much bigger than yourself. Tune in to the Earth's ecological seasons. Approach the world through patterns, and then use what you know to make predictions about what will happen next. Actively observe what's going on around you—fluctuations in wind, temperature, and light, and changes in familiar plant and animal life. Keep a systematic record of seasonal events, or *phenophases*. Note the first spring hummingbird and butterfly sighting, the first sign of ripe wild wineberries, the first stoneflies emerging from the neighborhood stream—all these phenophases are telltale signs of change and essential ingredients of growth. And all will help you predict when you'll see them again.

Things to Incorporate into Your Ecological Calendar

- Spring and fall equinox dates
- Summer and winter solstice dates
- Spring and fall frost dates
- Waxing and waning moon cycles
- Seasonal migratory bird and butterfly sightings
- Spring reemergence of crocuses, snowdrops, and earthworms
- First-of-season tadpole and snowfall sightings
- Vegetable garden planting and harvesting times
- Flowering dates of native trees like redbud, dogwood, and white ash
- First-ever sightings of gyrfalcons, double rainbows, and egg-laying monarchs
- Record-setting rainfall and extreme temperatures

EXPLORE MORE

There is constant change all around you, all the time. If you're patient enough to stay in one spot long enough, you'll witness complete metamorphosis right before your eyes. Even if you aren't camping out in Arizona's Grand Canyon, Hawaii's Mount Haleakalā, or Grundarfjörður, Iceland, you're in luck. Consider something that regenerates or transforms—watching a sunrise is perfect for this sort of thing. On a clear early morning, wake up while it's still dark and choose a good spot. Just find a comfortable east-facing perch, sit still, and watch the twilight slowly take over the sky. Listen to the chorus of birds waking up. Use what you learn to be more sensitive to other changes around you—a crocus flower closing at night, a luna moth emerging from a cocoon, an intertidal barnacle exposed to surf. Nothing appears the same from one moment to the next.

Become reacquainted with other ecological changes around you—things you may have recognized long ago, but have forgotten. Here are more ways to tune in to the big picture and see where you fit into the Earth's ecological shifts and cyclical patterns.

Other Dates to Keep Track Of

January 5	National Bird Day
February 2	World Wetlands Day
March 14	International Day of Action for Rivers
March 21	World Forestry Day
April 22	Earth Day
August 27	Sneak Some Zucchini onto Your Neighbor's Porch Day
September 22	World Car-Free Day
December 5	International Volunteer Day

CONDUCT A LONGITUDINAL STUDY. One observation of something taken alone may seem a bit insignificant and may not reveal much. A series of such observations taken over time, though, can provide important information. Take a series of "snapshots" of something in transition—a withering porch pumpkin, a blooming wildflower, a sprouting seed, an emerging moth. Choose when you'll collect systematic information—for one minute of every hour on a single day, or for one minute once a week at the same exact time. You decide. Just provide enough observations to give you an understanding of change over time. And understand that observing something is more than just "hanging out." Be a mindful, self-aware thing-watcher. Pay close attention. Look at different parts of the subject. Take detailed, nonjudgmental, concrete notes of what you see, hear, and smell.

LONGITUDINAL STUDY	TAKE DETAILED CONCRETE NOTES OF WHAT YOU SEE, HEAR, AND SMELL
DATE/TIME	OBSERVATION

OBSERVE A YEAR IN SOMEONE'S LIFE. Everything has its own timing, even plants. They have evolved ways to sense the passage of time—measuring day and seasonal length, and then diverting their energies to form flowers, seeds, and fruits, or to protect tender growing points and leaves within buds. Such sequential events are timed to match the seasons. Get to know the natural rhythms of a nearby tree. Pick one you can check on throughout the year. You can head to your backyard or a nearby park, but perhaps the best place to study a tree is in the woods. Pick a good tree—one that's especially good-natured and outgoing. Revisit your tree during different seasons, times of day, and weather conditions to investigate the changes that occur. Document your observations. Gather specific data.

A YEAR IN THE LIFE OF A TREE

Make a sketch of a leaf from your tree. Is it lobed? Heart-shaped? Triangular?	Remove the paper from a crayon. Place this page on the tree. Rub the side of the crayon along the paper. Make a bark rubbing of your tree right here.
If your tree is deciduous (broad-leaved), what is the date the leaves emerged in spring?	What is the flowering date of your tree?
How tall do you think your tree is?	Make a sketch of your tree's flower here. Note the color.

Play taxonomist. Use your own clues and a field guide to track down the species of your tree.

WRITE DOWN THE TREE SPECIES HERE:

_____

🌿**CHART THE PATTERNS OF TRANSITION.** Sometimes in life the rug gets pulled out from under your feet. And sometimes change happens because of choices you make. Situations can be thrown at you from all directions, and you may not respond in a predictable way. Life can be messy. This is the case with everybody. Even plants.

Dendrochronologists study past events by studying cross sections of tree trunks and comparing successive annual growth rings. Each successive layer consists of two colors of wood: light-colored *earlywood* that grows in warm months, and dark, denser *latewood* that grows in cool months. Although a tree makes a new ring every year, not every annual ring is the same. Variation in rings is mostly due to fluctuations in environmental conditions during growth. A tricky dry spell, a spike in a hungry insect population, an increase in shade—these are important events in a tree's life.

Consider the pattern of transitions in your own life. Starting with Point A in your own core, label each concentric circle with a major life transition as you journey toward Point B. If you're a seasoned pioneer like me, feel free to add extra rings.

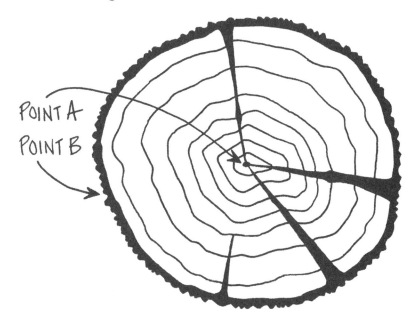

POINT A
POINT B

UNDERSTAND WORLDLY PATTERNS. There's a formal system of thought for studying natural patterns. It's called *math*. It pops up all over the place around you—in spiraling seeds, in branching twigs, in unfurling fern fronds—and it leaves a trail of clues for you to spot. We live in a world of static and fluid patterns, astounding evidence of the deep mathematical basis of the natural world. Numbers are fundamental to the way nature grows stuff, like a mysterious code that tells a developing fern or sunflower what to do next. The fantastic thing is that math provides a way for us to unlock many of nature's mysteries.

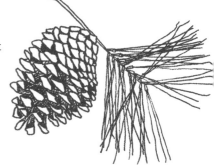

If you're a halfway curious person, at some point in your life you've probably inspected a pinecone or a daisy and pondered the magical pattern of its little parts. The amazing thing about a pinecone, a daisy, a sunflower, an artichoke, a pineapple, a this- tle, or a palm tree is that they all share the same intricate mathematical pattern. It's called the *Fibonacci sequence*. The neat thing about this sophisticated pattern is that it stems from a very humble beginning.

To understand it, you'll need to draw a perfect spiral on this graph pa- per. First, with a colored pencil or pen, trace the outline of Square 1, then Square 2 above it. You'll notice that the sides are the same length. The next (3) will have a length of Square 1 plus Square 2, the next (4) will have a length of Square 2 plus Square 3, and the next (5) will have a length of Square 3 plus Square 4. Keep spiraling around, adding larger and larger squares by adding up the lengths of the previous two squares (0 + 1 = 1, 1 + 1 = 2, 1 + 2 = 3, 2 + 3 = 5, 3 + 5 = 8, etc.).

When you've outlined all the shapes, add a curve (a *Fibonacci spiral*) going through each, moving from the southwest corner of Square 1 toward the northeast corner of Square 1, progressively arcing through each square, and linking each corner to its opposite corner. Resist the temptation to

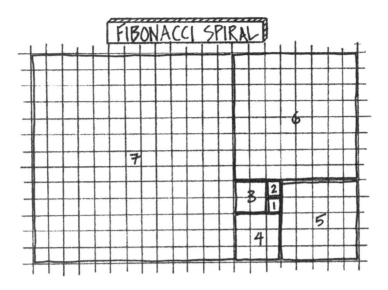

FIBONACCI SPIRAL

dash quickly across the diagonal—your spiral should be smooth and steady with no zigzag lines. On the graph, label each square with the length of its side. Write those numbers in a line here.

THE FIBONACCI SEQUENCE:

Now, search for something natural with a pattern—like a Brussels sprout stalk, pinecone, or Romanesco broccoli—and, starting with the base of the object, count the spirals going up to the right. Then count the spirals going up to the left. Chances are, these numbers will look familiar. They will fall somewhere within your Fibonacci sequence (. . . 5, 8, 13, 21, 34, 55, 89, 144 . . .). Now, step outside and zoom in on a flower. Count the number of petals. Most likely, the number of petals will also fall within your number series.

Be observant. You are sure to spot your spiral and the Fibonacci sequence in other unexpected places. There are patterns all around you. Be vigilant and you'll see them. Of course, there are other patterns in clouds, forests, leaves, and feathers—they are absolutely everywhere. Once you begin to see them, your view of the world will be forever changed. You'll discover patterns and sequences that seem too spectacular to be true, and then you'll prove to yourself that it's impossible for them *not* to be true.

THINGS FOUND WITH PATTERNS

OBJECT	NOTES

DOCUMENT IT

How Tuned in Are You? Rate Yourself

Check the box that most describes you.

Who Are You?

❑ I live and work in an underground bunker, and I survive on ready-made meals packed in airtight Mylar pouches.

❑ I'm an urbanite who works and plays indoors. My activities go on the same regardless of the weather. I pay my bills online and work nights compiling data on Bigfoot sightings. It doesn't matter if it rains or shines. Life is good.

❏ I know what season it is. Seasonal changes sneak up on me, though, and I adapt after the fact. I'm often unprepared for the day's weather. I'm constantly kicking myself—I'll grab my umbrella next time! I have a backyard birdfeeder, but it's mostly empty.

❏ I do seasonally appropriate things. On a warm day, I'll wear shorts and fire up the BBQ. I recognize a few backyard critters by sight or sound. I recognize poison ivy when I see it. I volunteer for cleanup days at our local trail system.

❏ I make major lifestyle changes depending on season. I fully participate in seasonal activities or have a seasonal job. I am a beachfront magician, whitewater-rafting guide, landscaper, or snowplow operator. I have a veggie garden and dream of tending backyard chickens.

❏ I live off the fat of the land. I am a farmer, rancher, or modern homesteader. My life is entirely dependent on climate and weather for all my daily needs and long-term survival. I feel a direct and immediate impact when my crops fail. I am hard-core.

Now, look hard at your answer, and then challenge yourself. From now on, make a point to work your way down the above list. Become responsible for your own personal evolution and maturation. Like everything else on Earth, you are not a fixed and finished object. You are influenced by other things— by an increasingly complicated and changeable world. Use nature as a model to gracefully navigate life's ups and downs. Be flexible to ebb and flow—be fluid and adaptable—rather than fixed to a script. As you move forward on your path, see yourself as part of the world. Begin to trust, once again, the subtle changes all around you. And find yourself within the big picture, aware of the wider world around you.

7

Think Like a
Scientist

All life is an experiment. The more experiments
you make the better.
—RALPH WALDO EMERSON

One of the funny things about having a brain is that most of the time you forget that it's there. But, as you squirrel-proof the birdfeeder, reassemble your broken tape measure, and consider designing the world's fastest go-kart, you and your brilliant brain are, in effect, experimenting with the world—considering possible explanations for how things work, examining cause and effect, tinkering with solutions, collecting data, and then using this stuff to refine your conclusions. Your entire day is filled with conscious and unconscious systematic decisions based on information you've carefully gathered—through trial and error—all quietly performed and stored within a 1.5 kg gelatinous mass upon your head. Science is shrouded in great erudition and jargon, but in reality the scientific method is at the heart of what you do every single day.

Stripped down to its essentials, science is just a method of figuring things out. Your brain knows this. An earmark on a book page, a paperweight on a stack of notes, a tweak to a beloved cooking recipe—you instinctively take opportunities to experiment and find simple solutions to problems. Science isn't just a collection of facts—rather it's a path toward understanding the world. And, given almost no fancy scientific knowledge, you can *think* like a scientist.

Lately, we've all gotten a bit lazy in our critical thinking. In a world of increasing complexity and uncertainty, we seem to be asking fewer and fewer questions, leaving that up to the "real" scientists. Scientific reasoning has been "outsourced" to those folks who presumably are experts. As a result, we've started thinking that we're separate from science—stigmatizing scientists as not like everybody else—and thinking that someone else has everything figured out for us. We've stopped thinking critically. And this makes it particularly tricky for us to pick out the world's phonies, magicians, and hardened criminals. We can easily get outfoxed. But in a world of social, economic, and environmental challenges, it's crucial for us to distinguish lies from truth.

It's time to regain your skepticism. It's time to question things, to reason, to make distinctions, to challenge your own assumptions, and to challenge the assumptions of others. Become engaged in your own learning about the natural world. Become environmentally literate—gain the knowledge, tools, and sensitivity required to properly address environmental problems. Understand the nuts and bolts of nature. Become a restless skeptical questioner, challenging the established beliefs. Be open-minded. Think for yourself, and arrive at conclusions based on facts. This gives you evidence to back yourself up.

Why? It's your responsibility. These scientific skills will serve you in all aspects of life—whether you're selecting dishwashing liquid or casting your vote in a high-stakes election. Your everyday choices about how you live your life greatly impact you and your environment. The ethical challenges of today's world must not be left to narrowly focused "experts" in the field. An engaged and informed society, with regular people making informed decisions based on facts, is the key to making sustainable change in the world.

See yourself as an agent of change in your everyday life. Think like a scientist. And think of the world as your laboratory.

↛ TRY THIS ↚

Bug Lotion

Insects are Earth's most abundant form of animal life. They were here millions of years before we were here, and they're destined to remain here long after we're gone. We're stuck with insects. I don't know if you've ever noticed this, but as we inadvertently drive species like the black-footed ferret and the Pacific pocket mouse to the verge of extinction, our most herculean efforts can't put even the smallest dent into a mosquito population.

Only a handful of all insects—fewer than 1 percent—are considered pests to humans, and still these play a leading role in a complex interdependent ecosystem. Although, to you, there appears to be no benefit to having pesky bugs like mosquitoes around, to a dragonfly nymph, mosquitofish, purple martin, or brown bat, the eradication of mosquitoes and other insects would be disastrous. It makes sense to emphasize nonchemical control measures to keep insects at bay. Unless you have a pet praying mantis perched on your shoulder, you may have to try out different options.

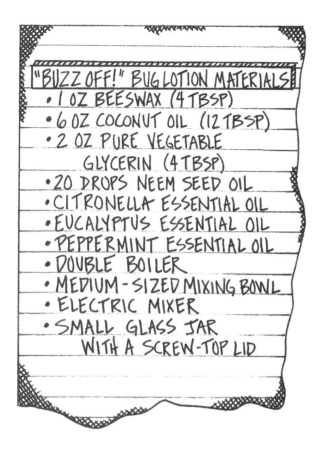

"BUZZ OFF!" BUG LOTION MATERIALS
- 1 OZ BEESWAX (4 TBSP)
- 6 OZ COCONUT OIL (12 TBSP)
- 2 OZ PURE VEGETABLE
  GLYCERIN (4 TBSP)
- 20 DROPS NEEM SEED OIL
- CITRONELLA ESSENTIAL OIL
- EUCALYPTUS ESSENTIAL OIL
- PEPPERMINT ESSENTIAL OIL
- DOUBLE BOILER
- MEDIUM-SIZED MIXING BOWL
- ELECTRIC MIXER
- SMALL GLASS JAR
  WITH A SCREW-TOP LID

Mix up a jar of this natural bug lotion to keep those biting bugs at arm's length. Experiment with different proportions of essential oils to see what does the trick.

PROJECT STEPS

STEP 1. Combine the beeswax and coconut oil in a double boiler over medium heat until the wax is melted (about ten minutes).

STEP 2. Remove the mixture from heat and add glycerin. Stir to combine.

STEP 3. Pour it into a medium-sized mixing bowl and beat well with an electric mixer, scraping sides, until creamy (about three minutes).

STEP 4. Add neem seed oil. Mix to blend.

STEP 5. Add a total of sixty drops essential oil blend—eucalyptus, citronella, and peppermint—to the mixture. Keep in mind that a combination of oils may be beneficial. Different oils repel different insects, and oil potency may be affected by the wearer's skin chemistry. In the end, it's up to you to determine the best proportions. Mix to blend.

STEP 6. Pour the mixture into a glass jar. Flatten the top of the lotion with a small spoon. Label the jar appropriately and store it out of reach of children. Use the lotion within a few months.

Be Safe!

Essential oils are aromatic liquids obtained from plant materials—flowers, buds, leaves, twigs, seeds, bark, and roots. They are highly concentrated. It takes about 200 liters of lavender flowers to make about 1 liter of essential oil. Never apply undiluted oils directly to your skin. And, as with any new skin product, always do a skin patch test to determine if you have an allergy to any ingredients. Dab a tiny amount of the bug lotion on your inner wrist and wait two days. If no rash appears, you are most likely not allergic to the ingredients. If you're pregnant or smallish, use extra caution when using or choosing es-

sential oils. Also, never use them near sensitive or broken skin, or around your eyes. Wash your hands thoroughly after each application. Do your research. Know what you're putting on your body, and take precautions. And when in doubt, consult a physician.

OH, THE SCIENCE OF IT ALL!

Natural Armor

Almost all organisms have evolved chemical or mechanical adaptations to avoid predation—noxious chemicals (like skunk spray), physical armor (like raspberry thorns and sea urchin spines), and cryptic coloration (like rattlesnake blotches) are just a few examples of antipredator adaptation. Plant-based repellents—mostly essential oils—can be harvested and incorporated into simple concoctions to make a natural armor against the bugs that really bug you.

Citronella, a common ingredient used in formulating natural commercial mosquito repellents, is a perennial "clumping" grass that emits a strong odor. Biting insects have antennae with *chemo-receptors* that detect lactic acid, carbon dioxide, and other volatile compounds released from the breath and skin of warm-blooded animals. Insect repellents with essential oils like citronella are believed to block the stimulation of these chemo-receptors, thus preventing insects from homing in on their source.

✦ NOW TRY THIS ✦

Consider a Risky Experiment

Scientists rely on their senses to gather information about the natural world, investigate phenomena, acquire new knowledge, and then make inferences using reason and logic. This technique, called the *scientific method*, is based on systematic observation, measurement, and experimentation. In effect, the scientific method attempts to minimize the influence of experimenter bias.

Now it's your turn to be a scientist. Take the first steps toward designing your own scientific experiment. Take a close look at a tiny backyard critter: the mosquito. Before you make any sort of scientific

Be Safe!

Before you head outside to observe your study organism, carefully consider your environment. Do not intentionally seek out sites teeming with frenzied female mosquitoes. Wear light-colored long sleeves and pants, and avoid swampy areas during mosquito rush hours—early morning and twilight. Please do not deliberately get bitten. There is a wide array of creepy mosquito-borne illnesses out there in the world. Be safe. I want you around for a while.

Mosquito Facts

What is the deadliest animal on the planet? The mosquito. Any number of humanity's most evil illnesses, including dengue fever, malaria, yellow fever, and encephalitis, are spread by its bite. It's been estimated that mosquito bites result in two to three million human deaths per year worldwide.

If a mosquito "bit" you, it was a female. She hatched and emerged from nearby water, collected nutrients in her diet from flower and plant nectar, and then used temperature, chemical, and visual cues to home in on you. She sensed your location up to 50 meters away. Her double-barreled proboscis probed your skin to find a blood vessel. She pierced your skin with two tubes—one sucked out some blood, and the other left behind a saliva drop. This drop contained an anticoagulant that induced an allergic response (an itchy, irritating bump called a *wheal*) within your skin. She used protein in your blood as an energy source for egg production. And in her brief life of just a few weeks, she laid one to three thousand eggs in nearby water. Wowza!

prediction, you must first make some direct observations of your study organism. This entails going outside and watching mosquitoes in their natural habitat. Don't skip this step in the scientific process. Even though you've probably met a mosquito before, you've never examined it through the keen eyes of a scientist.

After you've closely observed your study organism in action, you will most likely be inspired to ask some questions. Do mosquitoes ever sleep? What attracts a mosquito to somebody like me? Any question is a good question, and the great thing about any question is that it yearns for an answer, and it can launch serious scientific investigation.

It's time to suggest a possible answer to one of your questions in

Bug After-Bite

Just in case you *do* get a bug bite while observing mosquitoes . . . zap the itch with homemade after-bite. First, try not to scratch it, since you should not apply this to broken skin. Then, soak a cotton ball in *witch hazel* and apply it to the bite for a few minutes. The astringent tannins, procyanadins, resin, and flavonoids will help soothe pain and reduce swelling. Apply essential *camphor oil* with a cotton ball and wait for a minute. Camphor, mostly harvested from the wood of Asian camphor laurel trees and a common ingredient in commercial anti-itch gels, will stimulate your nerve endings and relieve your pain symptoms.

the form of a *hypothesis*—this is an educated guess based on your observations of mosquito behavior. Often expressed as an "If . . . then . . ." statement, a hypothesis is a prediction of what you think will happen. When a hypothesis involves a cause-and-effect relationship, it should be stated to indicate there is no effect. This is called a *null hypothesis*. For example, a null hypothesis concerning the effects of your new homemade bug lotion might be stated: "The type of essential herb in bug lotion will not affect the number of mosquito bites on my forearm."

Now take a stab at writing your very own hypothesis or null hypothesis about mosquitoes. Make a prediction about what you think will happen.

PREDICT WHAT WILL HAPPEN RIGHT HERE:

EXPLORE MORE

To start thinking of yourself as a scientist and become reacquainted with nature, you must consciously apply scientific habits of mind to the natural world around you—question what you observe, be open-minded, think creatively, and investigate further—your job is exploration of the real world, with no preconceptions. The following pages are filled with more ways you can hone your experimenting skills.

WHY ARE THERE NO GIGANTIC INSECTS? HOW DOES A STONE SKIP ACROSS A POND? WHY DON'T SPIDERS STICK TO THEIR OWN WEBS? WHY DO TOES WRINKLE IN THE TUB? WHY DO STARS TWINKLE? WHY DOES HAIR TURN GRAY? WHY DO WE DREAM? DO FISH DRINK WATER?

EXPLORE OUTSIDE THE LINES. I keep track of questions that I'll someday answer. I have many. Sometimes I stockpile them on pieces of scrap paper, and sometimes I stash them in my nature junk journal. It's your turn now. Join me. On the bee's trail, write down as many questions about the natural world you can think of—things you see every day and wonder about. Pick your brain. The way things almost always begin is innocuous and small. But, small things can spark big ideas for future scientific studies.

✍ MAKE A HYPOTHESIS. A hypothesis is a hunch. It's a statement of prediction that describes in concrete terms what you expect will happen, or what you think caused something to happen. If you've spent any time eavesdropping on the world, you often find yourself with a mystery on your hands that requires solving—a missing tube sock, a broken toaster, a UFO sighting—your hypothesis is your guess about causation based on what you already know. A single scientific study may, in fact, have several hypotheses. Write an "If . . . then . . ." statement in simple, clear language, such as: "If a tube sock goes missing every Friday afternoon, then my accordion teacher is the culprit."

Go outside and take a look around. Consider the unsolved mysteries of the natural world. Write down five clear hypotheses, keeping in mind that your statements should be testable through experimentation.

STATE FIVE TESTABLE HYPOTHESES ABOUT THE NATURAL WORLD:

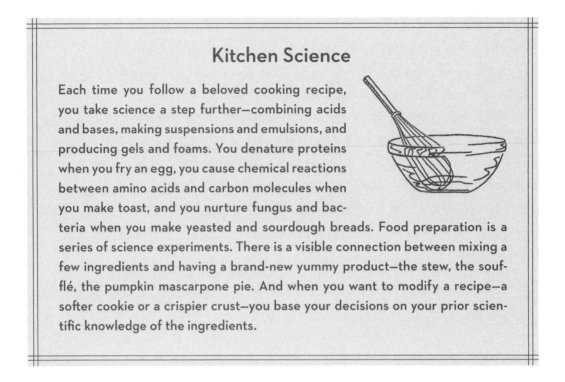

Kitchen Science

Each time you follow a beloved cooking recipe, you take science a step further—combining acids and bases, making suspensions and emulsions, and producing gels and foams. You denature proteins when you fry an egg, you cause chemical reactions between amino acids and carbon molecules when you make toast, and you nurture fungus and bacteria when you make yeasted and sourdough breads. Food preparation is a series of science experiments. There is a visible connection between mixing a few ingredients and having a brand-new yummy product—the stew, the soufflé, the pumpkin mascarpone pie. And when you want to modify a recipe—a softer cookie or a crispier crust—you base your decisions on your prior scientific knowledge of the ingredients.

DOCUMENT IT

The Undone Experiment

Choose one curious phenomenon in the natural world—a herd of deer repeatedly facing magnetic north, a water strider skimming across a pond's surface, a house wren sabotaging a bluebird nest—and think up a possible explanation for it. Come up with an experiment to test your theory. Create a meaningful title, form a hypothesis, and detail what information you plan to collect.

EXPLAIN YOUR EXPERIMENT IN THIS SPOT:

Continue to seek out inspiration in unlikely places—your kitchen, your garage, your backyard—and jump-start your experimentation engine. Do those things that incline you toward stirring investigations. Look at everything around you as an opportunity to ask more and more questions, and what might seem to be a series of unrelated events may in fact be the first steps of a scientific journey. Tinker with odds and ends. Take things apart, study them and test them. Learn what you can. Regain your skepticism. Look around and say to yourself, "I wonder why *that* happened." Treat each day as a treasure to unearth, each moment as a secret to discover. Make good choices based on evidence you yourself have gathered. Make mistakes. Mistakes can be useful. Think like a scientist. It's a complicated world, and you can never know what you don't know.

8

Harvest Something

Eat food. Not too much. Mostly plants.
—MICHAEL POLLAN

For perhaps a million years, humans survived on native plants and a handful of animals we could wrest from our own immediate environment. We ate what we could find. Then we built communities around food. Just a century ago, we'd get fresh pork from a butcher, butter from a local dairy farmer, and eggs and produce from the backyard, woods, or cellar larder. Almost everyone in the community took part in growing a harvest. Agricultural yields were modest, but stable. Seasonal crop rotations suppressed insects, weeds, and disease by breaking the life cycles of the pests. There was a solid bond between farming and ecology.

Today, we are patrons of the supermarket chain, a relatively new time- and effort-saving invention that offers us a year-round supply of just about anything. And, with the rise of big food retailers, we've lost our connection to food—where it comes from, how it grows and develops, what healthy soil feels like, how food should be prepared, and how we should dispose of extras—and we are paying the price.

Despite our near obsession with dieting, nutrition, and food-related television shows, we're facing a worldwide health crisis—a whopping surge in obesity, diabetes, and heart disease rates—most likely stemming from our relationship with what we eat. Food has become something that someone else grows and packages for us. There is a huge cultural divide between the farmer and the rest of society, and this distance enables us to make purchases without any knowledge whatsoever of the impacts of our decisions. It's a recipe for disaster.

How you choose to satisfy your appetite is an act that can greatly affect your own health as well as the health of the things around you. Supermarkets are in the business of encouraging you to purchase more food, and it can be tricky to make good choices when you're faced with so many flashy options. But if you can make responsible choices about what you put in your body, where it comes from, and how you prepare it and dispose of the extras, you'll benefit not only yourself but also the ecosystem on which all life depends.

You (yes, *you!*) determine how the Earth is used. This chapter will reveal the importance of cooking efficiently and eating fresh, seasonal, local food. Soon, you'll be eating affordably, responsibly, and well. Dig in! Each bite you take has the capacity to change the world.

Superfood Sprouts

A seed (or grain or legume) has many nutritional advantages, but most of the goodness is locked up and is inaccessible to you due to natural enzyme inhibitors. A newly sprouted seed, however, is like an open treasure chest. Its riches are ready and waiting for you to snack on.

Germinate a year-round supply of eco-friendly high-protein sprouts—a new harvest every week of fresh baby greens right in your own kitchen. Add an energizing crunch to each meal—soups, salads, sandwiches, dips—with just a few centimeters of countertop space.

It's easy to grow your own year-round mini crop—without concern for weather, weeds, soil, or pests. And when you do so, you can discover the joy of connecting to your food, knowing what you're eating, and growing your own.

PROJECT STEPS

STEP 1. Rinse the mason jar with equal parts vinegar and water.

STEP 2. Soak and rinse the seeds in fresh, clean water.

STEP 3. Measure the seeds. For most seeds, use about 2 teaspoons. Experiment with the amount—different seed types and sizes result in different yields.

STEP 4. Rinse the seeds in cool water.

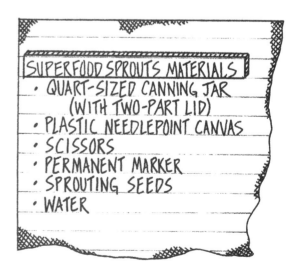

SUPERFOOD SPROUTS MATERIALS
- QUART-SIZED CANNING JAR (WITH TWO-PART LID)
- PLASTIC NEEDLEPOINT CANVAS
- SCISSORS
- PERMANENT MARKER
- SPROUTING SEEDS
- WATER

Choosing Sprouts

Sprouts are wonder foods. They rank as one of the freshest and most nutritious vegetables available and should be part of everyone's diet. Ounce for ounce, there are more nutrients in sprouts than any other food source. But, all sprouts are not equal. Taste, nutrition, and growing time vary. Head to your local health food store and select from this list of my favorite sprout varieties. Or, branch out and do your own research. There are so many to choose from.

Choosing Sprouts

VARIETY	FLAVOR	SOAKING TIME	SPROUTING TIME
Alfalfa	Nutty/Mild	8 hours	3 to 5 days
Broccoli	Mild to spicy	6 to 8 hours	5 to 6 days
Clover	Mild	4 to 6 hours	4 to 5 days
Radish	Spicy	4 to 6 hours	3 to 5 days

STEP 5. Place the seeds in the jar. Cover them completely with cool water, so that roughly 5 centimeters of water is above the seeds. Screw on the jar lid and place it in a cupboard out of direct sunlight. Soak the seeds for several hours (see "Choosing Sprouts" chart). The seeds will swell considerably as they absorb water and may be twice their original size afterward.

STEP 6. Remove the lid. With a permanent marker, trace the lid of the jar onto the plastic needlepoint canvas. Cut out the traced canvas circle. Replace the jar lid's inner metal disk with the canvas circle and screw the lid back onto the jar with the lid's metal ring.

STEP 7. Rinse the seeds with cool water until the water drains clear—two to three times.

STEP 8. Screw the lid onto the jar. Turn the jar upside down over the sink to drain. Shake the jar until the water is completely drained.

STEP 9. Find a spot with low light—a kitchen countertop is perfect for the job. Place the jar facedown at a slight angle. This allows fresh air to enter the jar and excess water to drain.

STEP 10. Rinse the seeds twice a day. Fill the jar with fresh cool water, swirl, and shake gently ten to fifteen seconds before draining. Repeat and then drain the excess water completely before returning the jar to its original upside-down tilted position. Repeat each day until the seeds fully germinate.

STEP 11. The amount of time it takes for a seed to fully germinate depends on the type of seed—it can take anywhere from a few hours to several days (see "Choosing Sprouts" chart). At this point, the seed coat ruptures and the seedling emerges—usually with the future plant root (or *radicle*) first. If you're antsy, you can stop at this point and move on to Step 12. Or, if you're patient, you can move the jar to a brighter spot—a windowsill with indirect light is perfect—to allow the sprouts to continue germinating for a few days. Continue to rinse the sprouts reg-

Be Safe!

- Be sure your purchased seeds are specifically labeled "sprouting seeds"— these are guaranteed to be pathogen-free.
- Keep everything sparkly clean.
- Be sure the sprouts are thoroughly dried and have plenty of air circulation.
- If you notice any sign of mold, compost the seeds and start fresh.

ularly, each morning and night. Never put your jar in direct sunlight unless you want scorched sprouts. Ick!

STEP 12. Harvesttime! When your jar is teeming with a tangle of sprout-lets, fill the jar with water and drain it thoroughly. Dry the seeds and store them in a clean glass container in the fridge. Eat them within one week.

OH, THE SCIENCE OF IT ALL!

Befriend a Sprout

While your sprouts emerge, get to know one really well. Pick a large one. Soak it for a day or two in water. Most likely, you can then slip off the outer covering, or *seed coat*. In a typical dormant flowering seed, like a bean or sunflower, there are two large parts (called *cotyledons*) protecting and nurturing the tiny plant (the *embryo*) within.

And what happens to lucky seeds—the ones that are actually planted? When a seed is ready to germinate, water is absorbed into the seed through a tiny hole within the seed coat. Rapid growth of the seed's embryo ruptures the seed coat, allowing the radicle to emerge in search of nutrients. The radicle becomes the *root* of the plant. The *hypocotyl*, the space between the radicle and the cotyledons, extends and emerges from the seed. Exposed to sunlight, the hypocotyl straightens out and develops into a *stem*. The cotyledons, now acting as two thick, leaf-like structures, become new green leaves. The tiny *plumule* rises up between the cotyledons and develops into the plant's *true leaves*. As you watch your seed grow up, identify its parts. Fill in this sketch along the way.

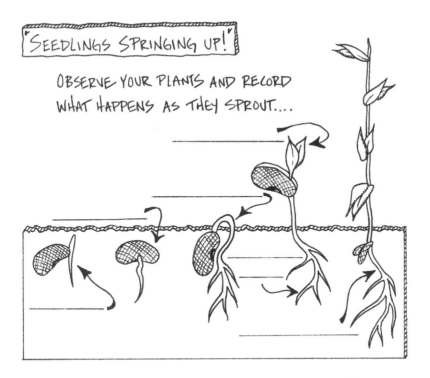

"SEEDLINGS SPRINGING UP!"

OBSERVE YOUR PLANTS AND RECORD
WHAT HAPPENS AS THEY SPROUT....

✦ NOW TRY THIS ✦

Plants from Scraps

It's both economical and eco-friendly to grow things from kitchen leftovers. The most effortless scrap plants are scallions, leeks, spring onions, and fennel. After using most of the greens, place the unused white root end in a glass jar with a little water—enough to cover the roots of the cutting, but not the top. Keep it on a kitchen windowsill and replace the water weekly. The leaves will continue to grow. Just snip off what you need each time you cook. Simple as that!

EXPLORE MORE

Whether you're a vegan, vegetarian, lessatarian, flexitarian, pescatarian, meatless Monday-er, omnivore, or mindfulivore, your food choices play a key role in the world around you. It takes ingenuity and time to reduce waste in a world that extensively advertises and packages things. And if it seems overwhelming at first, don't worry. Start with a realistic goal and then take baby steps to get there. It may take years to make a significant lifestyle change. Do what's right at a pace that works for you. Think of it as a long-term adventure!

Here are some tips for eco-friendly shopping, cooking, and eating to get you started. Consider how you might incorporate some of these practices into your day to make immediate and lasting change.

EAT REAL STUFF. Eat whole and unrefined foods straight-up. The closer you can get to food in its natural state, the better. Ideally, eat something without an ingredient list—apple, pear, or broccoli—and if it has a label, be sure to read it. Avoid the flashy prepackaged processed foods in the heart of a market—those that include things like refined sugars, binders, preservatives, high-fructose corn syrup, extracted oils, and bleached flour. While some of these ingredients are plant derived, they've been robbed of their original spunk. Take time to visit quiet unpretentious whole foods inhabiting the market's perimeter.

EAT LESS MEAT. Eat more fruits, vegetables, and beans—also nuts, whole grains, and high-protein pasta. Switch from a high-fat diet rich in animal protein and simple carbs to a whole-foods plant-based diet high in protein and plant-based complex carbs. Really, anything with a leaf is good. A well-structured, plant-based diet will meet all your body's needs, and it's the easiest way to eat.

COOK SIMPLY. You can cook extraordinary food very simply. Keep a stash of core ingredients on hand—superfoods like fresh sprouts, beans, lentils, broccoli, salmon, berries, yogurt, squash, green leafy vegetables, nuts, and seeds. Plan uncomplicated meals. Taste as you go.

KNOW WHERE YOUR MEAL COMES FROM. Trace your food back to its roots. Grow your own, or buy food from a local organic source—it's the ideal way to ensure that each meal is fresh and high quality and to ensure the longevity of small, ethical suppliers. Consider this: organic farming practices reduce pollution, conserve water, reduce soil erosion, increase soil fertility, and use substantially less energy. Grow and harvest your own crop, support a local farmers' market, or join a CSA (community-supported agriculture) co-op. Connect with people who grow and sell food. Think of yourself as a partner with them.

CHANGE YOUR DIET SEASONALLY. Your food travels a long way to get to your plate—often thousands of kilometers. Long-distance, large-scale transportation burns large quantities of fossil fuels and emits gobs of carbon dioxide and black carbon, major contributors to global warming. Because of limited growing seasons in most regions, it's virtually impossible to eat locally and in season 100 percent of the time. The next best thing is to purchase what's in season somewhere else, hopefully not too far away. In many situations, the closer that food is produced to its market, the less impact its total life cycle will have on the environment.

Use the harvest calendar on the following page for a quick reference on what's seasonal in your region.

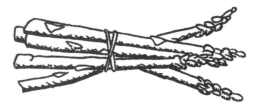

GROW SOME DIVERSITY. In the face of growing agricultural industrialization and genetic engineering, there's an urgent need to protect seed sovereignty—the right of the public to own and develop private seed supplies. Across the globe, new laws enforce compulsory registration of seeds, thus forcing small farmers into dependency on patented agricultural company seed, and making it impossible for small farmers to grow, save, and produce their own seed varieties.

To preserve genetic diversity and safeguard the integrity of our agricultural system, it's essential for you to consider a garden from a pioneer's perspective. Grow open-pollinated heirloom plants, harvest and save the seeds yourself, and exchange them with deserving friends and neighbors. Planting and replanting diverse high-quality heirlooms discourages monocrop culture and prevents the loss of unique varieties. Join a local seed co-op where you can obtain produce and wildflower seeds native to your distinct bioregion, and demand that public officials take a stand on reinvigorating old-school plant breeding and seed sharing.

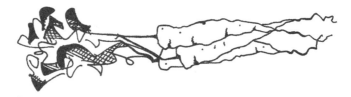

SEASONAL HARVEST CALENDAR

Mostly Western and Southern States	Mostly Northeast and Midwestern States
Spring Fruit: berries, cantaloupe, cherries, citrus, nectarines, papaya, passion fruit, peaches, plums, pluots, pomegranate, raspberries, rhubarb, strawberries	**Spring Fruit:** strawberries
Spring Vegetables: artichokes, asparagus, avocados, basil, beans, beets, broccoli, cabbage, carrots, cauliflower, celery, chard, collards, corn, cucumber, dates, eggplant, garlic, kale, kohlrabi, leafy greens, mushrooms, okra, onions, peas, potatoes, snow peas, spinach, squash, sweet peppers, tomatoes, turnips	**Spring Vegetables:** asparagus, fiddleheads, green onions, leafy greens, nettles, new potatoes, parsnips, radish, ramps, stinging nettles, wild mushrooms
Summer Fruit: apples, apricots, berries, cantaloupe, cherries, citrus, figs, grapes, melons, nectarines, passion fruit, peaches, pears, plums, pluots, strawberries, watermelon	**Summer Fruit:** blackberries, blueberries, boysenberries, cantaloupe, cherries, nectarines, peaches, pears, plums, pluots, raspberries, strawberries
Summer Vegetables: asparagus, avocados, basil, beans, beets, broccoli, cabbage, carrots, cauliflower, celery, chard, collards, cucumbers, eggplant, kale, kohlrabi, leafy greens, mushrooms, okra, onions, peas, potatoes, spinach, squash, sweet corn, sweet peppers, tomatoes	**Summer Vegetables:** asparagus, basil, beans, beets, broccoli, cabbage, carrots, chard, corn, cucumbers, eggplant, garlic scapes, kale, kohlrabi, leafy greens, onions, peas, potatoes, radishes, ramps, rhubarb, squash, sweet peppers, tomatoes, wild mushrooms
Fall Fruit: apples, berries, cantaloupe, citrus, cranberries, dates, figs, grapes, kiwifruit, melons, papayas, peaches, pears, persimmons, plums, pluots, pomegranate, prunes, strawberries, watermelon	**Fall Fruit:** apples, blueberries, cantaloupe, cranberries, grapes, melons, nectarines, peaches, pears, plums, pluots, prunes, raspberries, watermelon
Fall Vegetables: artichokes, asparagus, avocados, basil, beans, beets, Brussels sprouts, cabbage, carrots, celery, cucumbers, peppers, kale, kohlrabi, leafy greens, mushrooms, onions, peas, potatoes, spinach, squash, sweet corn, tomatoes, turnips	**Fall Vegetables:** basil, beans, beets, broccoli, Brussels sprouts, cabbage, carrots, cauliflower, chicory, cucumbers, celery, chard, corn, endive, fennel, eggplant, garlic, gourds, kale, kohlrabi, leeks, leafy greens, onions, parsnips, peas, potatoes, pumpkin, radish, rutabaga, sweet peppers, squash, tomatoes, turnips, wild mushrooms
Winter Fruit: citrus, dates, kiwifruit, pears, persimmons	**Winter Fruit:** cold storage apples and pears
Winter Vegetables: asparagus, avocados, beets, broccoli, Brussels sprouts, cabbage, carrots, cauliflower, celery, chard, dates, kale, kohlrabi, leafy greens, mushrooms, onions, peas, potatoes, squash, sweet potatoes, turnips	**Winter Vegetables:** beets, cabbage, carrots, kale, onions, parsnips, potatoes, pumpkins, squash, turnips, vegetables from root cellars and cold storage

STRIVE FOR ZERO WASTE. On average, the kitchen generates the most waste of any room in your house. Consider all the organic waste you produce in your kitchen and try to minimize what you put in the garbage. Leftovers can be eaten as is, frozen and reheated, or reinvented as new dishes. When all else fails, compost it. If it must be tossed, put it to good use in the garden.

DOCUMENT IT

Connect with What You Eat

Most of us eat out of habit without really thinking about what we're putting into our bodies. Consider what you eat and drink. Consider the origin of your food. Consider where it was packaged. Keep track of what you put into your body for one full day. Record all the ingredients on the next page—include everything on each label.

At the end of the day, examine the list. Is it long? The shorter the list, the better. Are there ingredients you don't recognize—anti-caking agents, artificial and natural flavors, emulsifiers, food colors, flavor enhancers, preservatives, sweeteners, stabilizers, and texturizers? Do some research. Determine what they are and if they should be avoided. Know what you eat and make conscious changes to your diet. Take into account the path your food took to get to your plate. Did things travel far? Are there local sources of these foods? If so, consider alternatives. Make informed decisions about what you buy and bite into. Eat well!

INGREDIENT LIST FOR ONE FULL DAY:

KEEP TRACK OF
EVERYTHING YOU
EAT TODAY

9

Make a Humble Home

Where thou art, that is home.
—EMILY DICKINSON

What makes a home? In nature, a home is simple. Ant formicary, spiderweb, squirrel drey, and insect gall—all are designed to provide shelter, and most are not elaborate. For animals, a home is not the stuff inside it. It is much more than that. It is a feeling and a way of being.

Until fairly recently, we followed a similar model. It was merely a century ago that a typical frontier home was built of sod or timber logs and sparsely furnished with handmade or repurposed items. Just outside the front door grew herbs and spices, a vegetable garden, and an orchard. Homestead geese and hogs grazed in the nearby woods. There was little use for money. We were self-sufficient—bartering with neighbors, repairing broken tools ourselves, making items we needed. We whipped up our own soap, candles, clothing, shoes, and furniture. Things we couldn't make—dishes, iron tools, gunpowder—were often exchanged for goods or services. We concentrated on basic survival—simple and manageable stuff. We danced lightly around the land and had little long-term impact on natural resources.

In this day and age, however, we often equate our elaborate homes with the "stuff" inside them. Some of that stuff is small, like a subway token, and some stuff takes up lots of space like a pinball machine. We hire "experts" to weed the garden; mend clothing; clean gutters, windows, and bathrooms; and organize all of our possessions. We sort stuff, catalog and maintain stuff, or stash stuff under the bed, all of which requires roomier rooms, supersized dwellings, and bigger beds. We live large lives, crammed with keeping up with the items we buy. And while each individual purchase seems fairly innocuous in its time and space requirements, having lots of possessions can get us terribly off track. Our prolonged overconsumption has enormous personal and social consequences—not to mention severe environmental ramifications. Much of what we consume slips casually into the garbage, producing a gargantuan amount of trash—so much so it's hard to imagine.

Turns out, it just so happens that a big, flashy house with lots of stuff crammed into it doesn't necessarily make a home. Instead, try keeping the spirit of the early pioneer's minimalism as an ideal. Concentrate on what is essential. Your lifestyle choices have a significant impact on your ecological footprint. Live small in your relationship with the natural world. Bear in mind that whittling your things down to the bare essentials is of little value if it's not a natural consequence of much deeper feelings—a reaction to understanding that you belong to something much bigger than yourself. In this way, the smaller you live compared to the vast wild world around you, the closer you come to being part of nature.

Start to work against the pressure for more stuff and start thinking about the idea of owning less stuff. Consider basic survival—horse, axe, cooking pots, corn, hoe, and bedroll—with a modern twist. Focus on the simple things—clean sheets, a hot shower, fresh food, a happy family, and a good book—and purge the excess. Reassess your needs and wants. You don't have to replace your pillow-top Sleep Number bed with a bearskin rug. Just make your life manageable with a minimum of necessities.

Could you live in a small sod frontier house? A cliffside shack hanging over a deep river-cut canyon? A weather-beaten cardboard bungalow? A log cabin? A three-blanket lean-to? A bird's nest? Maybe, if it was carefully constructed and filled up with warmhearted friends and a small handful of the right things. Put yourself in a home that fits well. Fill it with things that really matter.

In this chapter you'll see: small really *is* beautiful.

TRY THIS

Bird Nesting Ball

Perhaps the secret to leading a small, simple life is found right under your nose. A bird has never settled on a branch and asked herself: "Where did all this junk come from?" She keeps her small home nice and tidy and safe, filling it only with things that really matter: youngsters. She has no time for extras.

Use nature as a template. Discover the riches contained in a simple life. Provide a healthy supply of nesting material for a backyard bird or two. Present them with a homemade hand-packed nesting ball—materials hung in a handy bird-friendly dispenser—and watch the evolution of carefully constructed simple homes. Perhaps this will help you reassess your needs and wants.

BIRD NESTING BALL MATERIALS
- WILD GRAPEVINE
- SCISSORS
- PRUNING SHEARS
- TWINE OR RIBBON
- NESTING MATERIAL

Note: *Nesting material must be easily transported in a tiny beak. It can be as simple as a collection of tiny twigs. A more ambitious selection could include yarn scraps, hay, feathers, hemp, fibrous bark, nonmetallic ribbon, cotton scrap, pet hair, milkweed or cattail fluff, moss or lichen, broom bristles, wool, or bits of twine. Consider upcycling the offshoots of crafting projects, but be certain to omit dryer lint, synthetic material, or anything chemically treated. All items should be no wider than 2 centimeters, and no longer than 10 centimeters.*

PROJECT STEPS

STEP 1. Cut a fresh wild grapevine to measure approximately 1 meter. Use pruning shears to clip any rough stubble off the vine. If the vine is not completely pliable, completely submerge it in warm water to soak overnight. The next day it will still be stiff but flexible.

STEP 2. Stretch the vine out on an outdoor table or fence to remove excess water. Shape the vine into a hollow sphere measuring 15 centimeters, leaving some space between wraps and tucking both ends in. It should look like a hollow ball of twine. Allow it to dry in a safe spot for several days.

STEP 3. Select nesting material and cut it to desired length.

STEP 4. Weave the items among the gaps in the ball and stuff some materials into the center, teasing out tail end bits for tiny beaks to grab. Think like a bird. Cover the surface of the ball with a good selection of scraps, being careful that the items are not too snug or too loose.

STEP 5. Attach a long twine or ribbon to the ball and secure it to a

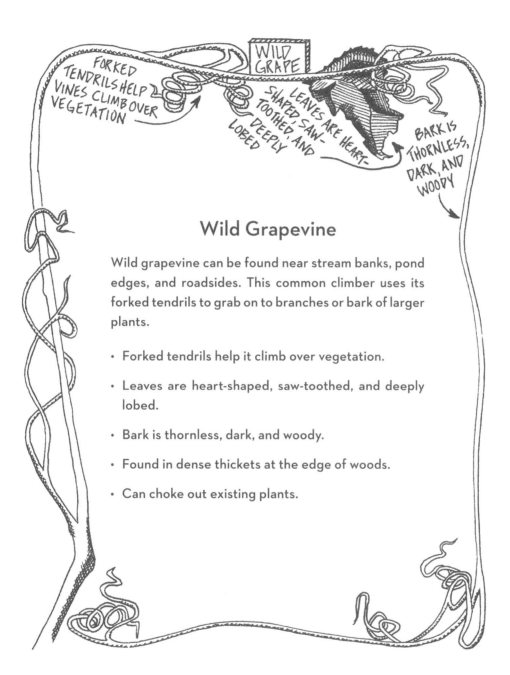

FORKED TENDRILS HELP VINES CLIMB OVER VEGETATION

WILD GRAPE

LEAVES ARE HEART-SHAPED, SAW-TOOTHED, AND DEEPLY LOBED

BARK IS THORNLESS, DARK, AND WOODY

Wild Grapevine

Wild grapevine can be found near stream banks, pond edges, and roadsides. This common climber uses its forked tendrils to grab on to branches or bark of larger plants.

- Forked tendrils help it climb over vegetation.

- Leaves are heart-shaped, saw-toothed, and deeply lobed.

- Bark is thornless, dark, and woody.

- Found in dense thickets at the edge of woods.

- Can choke out existing plants.

branch—a sheltered but visible location where birds frequent. A safe, quiet place. Over time, watch as neighborhood birds take beakfuls of odds and ends to construct new homes. And don't be surprised if a nice simple nest pops up soon in your backyard.

Note: *If wild grapevine is not available, use a clean suet basket or an empty mesh produce bag. Premade grapevine spheres are also widely available in craft stores. If you opt to use a produce bag that's open on both ends, tie one end closed with twine. Loosely fill the bag and tie the top with twine, leaving at least 1 meter of twine for hanging. Additionally, you may scatter nesting material on the ground, rub it into clingy tree bark, drape it gently over shrubs, cram it in tree crevices or spaces within a stone wall, or place it in hanging baskets.*

OH, THE SCIENCE OF IT ALL!

Homes Within Habitats

Bird nests are marvels of architecture, built with specific materials and meticulously maintained. Even an ostensibly simple nest is often elegantly constructed. A yellow warbler's nest may have coarse twigs at the base, finer plant fibers and grasses intertwined with weeds and plant stems inside the open cup, and plant down and wool within the inner lining. A more intricate nest, such as that of the Baltimore oriole, may require actual plant fiber weaving or knot-tying to secure materials.

Nest-building materials are also species specific—mud, silk, feathers, milkweed and cattail fluff, deer hair, lichen, spider silk, moss, twigs, leaves, petioles, roots, stones, flowers, seeds, ferns—each is carefully selected for unique nest-building tasks. For example, the great crested flycatcher often adds a piece of shed snakeskin to the nest to help deter predators or other intruders. Many hummingbird species use spiderwebs in their nests to make them pliable enough to expand as the nestlings grow within. Most birds are opportunistic builders, though, and will gladly integrate substitutes of similar size and texture into their nests.

☼ NOW TRY THIS ☼

Know Your Feathered Neighbors

Can you believe there are over ten thousand species of birds in the world? A handful of them can be found right where you live. With practice, these birds can be identified by sight.

Head outside and find a comfy place to quietly sit. Watch the surrounding ground and trees. Chances are some feathered friends will stop by. Take detailed field notes on special features—their song, plumage, shape, size, and behavior. Often what you think is an unimportant detail turns out to be the key element to properly identifying a species—like the wag of an eastern phoebe's tail. Just like somebody you meet once at a party and want to remember, take note of quirky habits and characteristics that stand out.

Once you return home, grab a local bird guide—your library should have a good one—and take a peek through it. Try to identify a few birds using your own clues. But, don't worry if you can't determine the names of any. That's not important. What *is* important is that you

What's That You Hear?

There's something to be said about "seeing" a bird with closed eyes. A good birder can determine a species just by hearing their call or song. Some species like the cedar waxwing have just one single simple call. Others, like the brown thrasher, can sing more than two thousand songs. No kidding! Learning bird songs takes patience, perseverance, persistence, and a great deal of practice. Here are some tips to help you along the way:

- Plug away at one or two common local birds first. Use these calls and songs as the standard for subsequent ones you hear.
- On busy spring days when there are many birds calling, consider each call as a separate instrument in a large orchestra. Tune in to individual notes from one single instrument, not the entire orchestra. Pick out the piccolo, then the oboe, the cello, and then the bass.
- Imitate the songs. If you can, count the number of notes, and sketch the bird and the melody. Do the notes rise? Do they fall?
- Use gimmicks, or *mnemonics*. If a bird sounds like a perky R2D2, then take note of it. You can use your own mnemonics, assigning your own words to a bird's song, or you can use widely accepted ones. As you identify backyard birds, add your own mnemonics to the list. But, remember—most species have many different calls. And, depending on where you live, you may be surrounded by different species making different sounds.

USEFUL MNEMONICS

Bubble, bubble, glee-gleek	Cowbird
Cheer-a-lee, cheer-up....	Robin
Chirping trill (mechanical)	Chipping sparrow
Chirping trill (softer than Chipping sparrow)	Dark-eyed junco
Conk-a-ree	Red-winged blackbird
Wich-ity, witch-ity, witch-ity	Common yellowthroat
Whinny (downward)	Downy woodpecker
Whinny (evenly pitched rattle)	Hairy woodpecker
Wik, wik, wik, wik, wik, wik	Flicker
Wolf whistle, squeaky squeal, clucks	Starling
Who are you, you, you (sadly)	Mourning dove
Yenk, yenk yenk (with a stuffy nose)	White-breasted nuthatch
Zeee-zeee zeee (high-pitched crickets)	Cedar waxwing

recognize the *features* of some of the birds you've seen. The next time you head outside, attempt to spot them again.

EXPLORE MORE

Put the brakes on mindless consumption. Curb your appetite. Relearn the essentials of living. Simplify your relationships, money, and time, and extricate yourself from the snarls of an overly complicated life. Get rid of superfluous things. Know what it is you value, learn how to spend time and money on essential things, and practice saying no to everything else. Learn how to have a big life within a small simple space. Here are additional ways to whittle yourself down.

BUILD YOUR NEST. Constructing your own simple home requires that you choose the specific building materials and contents wisely. Consider central recurring themes in your life—concepts, patterns, significant sounds, smells, tastes, or sensations that you can't help but be drawn toward in a positive way—things like your grandma, whitewater kayaking, the sweet smell of a wet dog, or Indian classical music. Then whittle things down to what's important. Focus on the lifelong patterns that are the core of your being. These are the things your nest should be built with, as they're strong and familiar to you, and will provide a safe shelter for whatever winds up inside.

What will you put in your nest? It will be very small, so you should think like a minimalist. You wouldn't want to encumber yourself with too much, but certainly you wouldn't want to forget to include the important stuff (like close friends, Orpington chickens, kabocha squash pie, or this book). Hold on to what's essential and place it carefully into your nest; weed out what's not important. Take the time to remove the clutter in your life and you'll be left with something much more amazing than before.

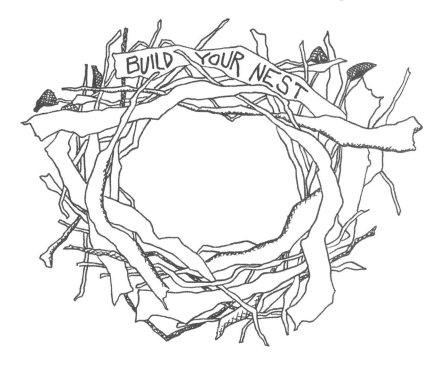

🌿 **SWAP FAVORS.** To get rid of extras, early settlers often relied heavily on bartering. They worked with what they had, trading goods and services without the use of money. The wheat farmer would trade surplus yield to the blacksmith in exchange for the repair of a shovel plow. With the restored plow, the farmer enjoyed an increased harvest and could barter with others—the shoemaker, basket maker, or gunsmith—to trade more and more stuff.

This ancient practice is far from defunct. It's all around you in nature—you see it in the alliance between figs and wasps, legumes and soil bacteria, plant roots and fungi, and ants and aphids. It's part of your own life as well—that yam and jam muffin you traded for your friend's Twinkie? Bartering.

In a quest to simplify your home, take advantage of bartering. Trade items you *don't* want for services you *do* want. Consider what items you are willing to offer, assess the dollar value of your goods, find a trading partner, and hammer out the details. An ongoing deal (like a steady supply of fresh garden squash in exchange for weekly babysitting) should always be put in writing. The value of something is relative. It depends on a person's wants and needs.

Plan out your bartering future.

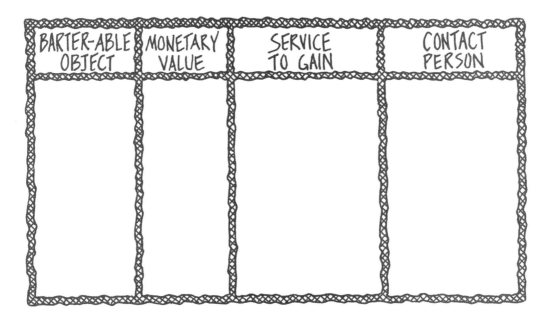

BARTER-ABLE OBJECT	MONETARY VALUE	SERVICE TO GAIN	CONTACT PERSON

🌱 **GROW INDEPENDENT.** You don't need a brood of laying hens or a backyard cow to become a more self-sufficient homesteader. Just keep basic repair tools at your disposal—like a cast-iron skillet, claw hammer, power drill, duct tape, and sewing kit—so you're able to jump right in and fix beat-up and broken items. Consider making and growing things yourself—baking bread, sprouting kitchen herbs, or growing fresh vegetables. Although at first this may seem to complicate things, in the end you'll benefit. You'll save money by not paying potential "experts," and you'll gain a sense of pride in what you've accomplished. Re-caulk the tub, mend your own clothes, weed your garden, unclog your own drain. Reduce your reliance on folks outside your home. Simplify.

MOVE FROM TRASH TO TREASURE. Downsize. In your quest for uncomplicated living, give any leftovers away. Your extra odds and ends are likely to be cherished by somebody else out there. Did your neighbor make eyes at your lawn flamingo? Now, *there's* a perfect match. Find new homes for things you no longer need. Hitch them up with appreciative people. No need to go militant with a decision to own only thirty items that will fit in your saddlebag. Just eliminate unnecessary things. Make a plan to give away one item every day for one entire week. If you have accoutrements popping out of drawers, closets, and windows, though, feel free to continue way past then.

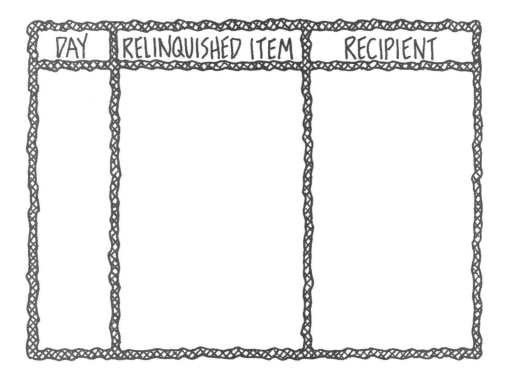

DAY	RELINQUISHED ITEM	RECIPIENT

DOCUMENT IT

What Makes a Home?

When does a house become a home? Is it when someone's height is marked on its kitchen wall? Or when a planted sapling begins to shade it? Or when the first neighbor is met? Or when a beloved hamster is buried in its back garden? Or when an unanticipated popcorn eruption and ignition sets off the smoke alarm? What makes *your* house a home? Carve your answers carefully into the floor.

Continue to reassess your needs and wants and purge your life of the inessential. Strip yourself of everything that entangles you, and relearn the essentials of living. Know what it is you value. Look at all the good things you already have. These are the things that should fill your life. In your quest for simple living, perhaps you'll find the secret to happiness lies right under your nose.

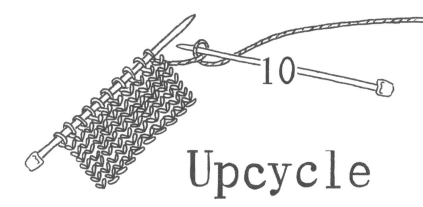

10

Upcycle

Use it up, wear it out, or do without.
—NEW ENGLAND PROVERB

🌱

In nature, nothing is wasted. When a plant dies, it decomposes and becomes the nutrients for new life. A host of creatures, including soil invertebrates, fungi, and bacteria, physically break up the plant material into its constituent chemicals. These diligent decomposers produce energy and waste, thus returning nutrients to the soil. The roots of living plants then take up these nutrients, enabling the establishment of new seedlings. Organic material is naturally recycled. It's a closed loop. There are no leftovers.

Until fairly recently, humans followed a similar model. Just a century ago, almost every bit of house, kitchen, shop, or farm scrap was reused, remade, traded, or simply pitched out the window to be eaten by an enterprising pig. Packaging was reused—grain sacks became curtains, barrel hoops became toys, crates became chairs.

The idea of waste as we know it today is a

recent concept. It's impossible to overstate the future ramifications of our modern throwaway, disposable, drive-through lifestyles. In reality, things don't die and vanish when they're thrown out. They live on and on. And so, amid alluring advertisements for fragranced electric air fresheners, flashy banana slicers, spinning spaghetti forks, and vinyl-cloaked bubbly drain cleaners, you should consider every day what you purchase and throw away. Always consider what happened before you got there and what will happen next. Look to nature as a guide. Consider packaging. Buy in bulk. Multiple uses are better than single uses. Reduce, reclaim, refurbish, repair, reuse, recycle, repurpose, and donate—the world has thrived on these techniques for millions of years on its own. It's time to return to a life without so many leftovers.

This chapter will inspire you to live prudently and to upcycle—to take something that would otherwise end up in a landfill and make it into something that has equal or greater value. The real trick is to upcycle natural things you already have on hand. Seek out opportunities right under your nose—castoffs bound for the garbage. Transform a burlap coffee sack into a throw pillow, a shipping pallet into a shoe rack, dryer lint into modeling clay, a newspaper page into a seedling pot, a road map into a stack of envelopes—these things are usually biodegradable and can later decompose when they are over the hill. With a little elbow grease, you can mimic the natural processes and transform something lifeless into something truly amazing.

⇥ TRY THIS ⇤

A Flower in Sheep's Clothing

It has been said that life's mistakes are like pebbles that make a good road, meaning not that great roads are bumpy, but that unfortunate accidents in life can often be used as stepping-stones to a new idea that might not have otherwise been discovered. The felted flower is like that. It begins with a mistake and there's really no way to mess up the outcome. It's not unlike making lemonade out of lemons. Few things are as satisfying as using sheer ingenuity to turn a bad situation into a good one.

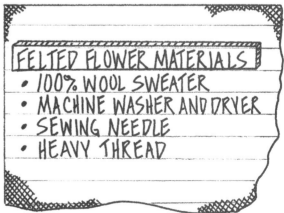

But upcycling is more than that. The best thing about almost any upcycling project like this one is that the thing you wind up with is significantly more amazing than the thing you start with. Based on the idea of making stuff last as long as possible while in someone's hands, upcycling is about giving an object a long, happy life. It's about intentionally improving the quality of something and then using it until it's completely worn out. Try doing this with an old wool sweater.

PROJECT STEPS

STEP 1. Gather up the supplies. Choose an old wool sweater that you've unintentionally washed and shrunk, or select a few shabby unshrunk sweaters you're willing to retire—not the hand-knit ones from your Great Aunt Opal. They should be medium-weight sweaters—not too thick or too thin. I'm often partial to snazzy colors—luminous greens, saucy oranges—although, surprisingly, humble grays and browns can be just as powerful.

STEP 2. Grab a load of laundry and add your sweaters to the batch (see "Felting Tips"). Wash the load in hot water and dry it thoroughly in the dryer with everything else. Afterward, your sweaters will be slightly smaller and thicker than they were previously. You've felted them. And, look at that! You've done the laundry!

FELTED FLOWER MATERIALS
- 100% WOOL SWEATER
- MACHINE WASHER AND DRYER
- SEWING NEEDLE
- HEAVY THREAD

Felting Tips

What makes a good sweater to upcycle? When considering what sweaters to felt, 100 percent wool is easiest. Other animal fibers like mohair, cashmere, and alpaca will work as well, though. Be sure the tag is not labeled "superwash," since this washable wool will have been chemically treated to avoid shrinkage (i.e., felting). Remove all buttons, ribbons, labels, etc. from the sweater, cut it apart at the seams (completely cutting away the stitched seam), and toss it into the hot-water wash and cold-water rinse with the laundry pile. Wash everything with biodegradable laundry detergent or soap and pop everything in a hot dryer until completely dry. Often, I wash and dry my sweaters twice to ensure shrinkage.

STEP 3. Prepare the "petals" for the project. With sharp sewing scissors, cut the felted sweaters into long zigzaggy strips with pointy or rounded tops, leaving a connection on the bottom edge. Cut smooth, fine sweaters into narrow strips for inner petals, and bulky sweaters into wide strips for outer petals.

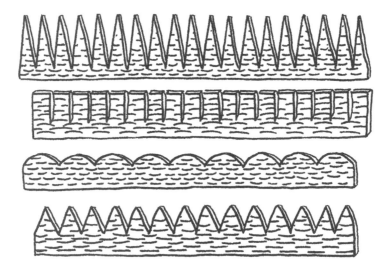

STEP 4. Make the flower center. Cut a long strip of sweater material—approximately 15 cm × 1.5 cm. With needle and long thread in hand, roll the fabric into a tight chunky cylinder, like a pinwheel cookie, and stitch it together. Pass the thread through the center and out the other side several times. Secure and cut the thread.

STEP 5. Stitch the bottom edge of one narrow petal strip around the sides of the flower center until it reaches the starting point. Trim the extra end of the strip. Stitch a thicker petal strip around the sides of the flower, matching bottom edges and overlapping the first strip until it reaches the starting point. Trim the end. Stitch a third (the widest and bulkiest) petal strip around the first two. Trim the end off the strip and secure and cut the thread.

STEP 6. Cut a 6 cm × 3 cm leaf-shaped piece of felted sweater material. Place this piece on the bottom of your flower and sew around the edges, covering all untidy bits of the flower's underside. Don't attempt floral perfection. Instead, bask in the glory of quirkiness. Remind yourself that, in nature, some flowers are smaller, some are fatter, some grow to the left, some to the right, and some even lose petals along the way.

STEP 7. Secure a hair tie or safety pin onto the leaf bottom with needle and thread. Alternatively, to permanently showcase your crafty accomplishment, consider sewing your upcycled felted flower directly to a lapel, hat, or mitten.

OH, THE SCIENCE OF IT ALL!

Wool Felting

Felt is a mass of dense wool and/or fur. It is not woven, but rather pressed and manipulated in a centuries-old process using heat, moisture, and pressure or agitation. The result: the strongest, smoothest, most water-resistant natural fabric known. Soap helps in the felting process. Heat and moisture cause the outer overlapping scales along the wool fiber to open, and the soap allows the fibers to slide easily over one another, thereby causing

Mad Hatters

Since wool felt is not woven and doesn't require a loom for its production, it can be made rather easily. Because of this, felt is the earliest known form of fabric. The true origin of felt is unknown, though several cultures take credit for its discovery. One Sumerian legend tells of Saint Clement, a wandering monk, who cleverly wrapped flax fibers between his shoes and feet to prevent blisters. Upon arrival at his destination, he removed his shoes to discover that the flax had, in fact, felted due to heat, pressure, and perspiration. Saint Clement became the patron saint for hatmakers.

The steps included in making felt have changed little over time. Felted fabric is produced using heat, moisture, and pressure to mat and interlock the fibers. While machinery can be used today to accomplish many of these tasks, the processing requirements remain unchanged. One exception is that until the late nineteenth century mercury was used in the processing of felt for hat making. Mercury was discovered to have debilitating effects on the hatter, causing a type of poisoning that led to tremors, hallucinations, and other psychotic symptoms—hence the term "mad hatter."

them to become entangled. Wool fibers are made up of a protein called *keratin*. The keratin in the fibers becomes chemically bound to the protein of the other fibers resulting in a permanent bond between the fibers. The felting process is irreversible. Sometimes this is unfortunate. You may have a closet brimming with unintentional pint-sized sweater casualties on hand as silent reminders.

Felt made with a thrifted sweater has all the benefits of wool—stability, durability, earthy texture—and has the eco-friendly attributes of being natural and secondhand.

✦ NOW TRY THIS ✦

Alternative Upcycling

Once you've chopped up and felted a sweater or two, and you've got the felted flower under your belt, take your pile of felted sweater scraps a step further. There are plenty of other ways to transform and reuse old sweaters. Want to add more character to your sweater stash? Spread the word and collect unwanted wool bits from friends and neighbors. Stitch different scraps together, add embellishments, and give rise to an almost infinite variety of upcycled things. Here's a list of just a few ideas for upcycling inspiration:

Alternative Upcycled Sweater Projects
* Newborn hat, blanket, and bunting
* Teapot or wine cozy
* Baby leggings and booties
* Pincushion
* Winter scarf and mittens
* Fingerless gloves
* Earmuffs

- Drink coasters
- *Flashdance* leg warmers
- Hand puppets
- Miniskirt
- Crazy quilt
- Throw pillow
- Lamp shade
- Sewing basket
- Journal cover

EXPLORE MORE

Create less waste by nudging your daily behaviors into more sustainable routines and expectations. Be conscious of the waste you create. Consider the lifecycle of familiar objects. Consider how things got here and where they are going. Here are more ways to work against the tide of trash.

LIBERATE YOUR LITTER. An object's lifespan depends entirely on the life of its constituents. The ecological impact of an object can be determined by evaluating the degradability of the object's compounds within the environment. In the natural world, different materials biodegrade at different rates. What's the lifespan of a banana peel? Two weeks. A newspaper? Six weeks. A birdseed bag? Twenty years. A fishing line? Eight hundred years. A plastic jug? One million years. A polystyrene cup? Maybe forever.

Consider the history and future of a discarded object. Pick through your recycling bin or donation pile and select something that still has some spunk. No need to turn a jerry can into rolling luggage, a collection of Pez dispensers into a menorah, or a stack of telephone directories into a prom dress. Just begin with something basic and tap into your imagination. Upcycle just one object you already own into something completely different. Make a dozen envelopes out of an old map, a placemat out of an old bag, or a marble maze out of toilet paper rolls, and you will see. There's something about making something from something.

🌿 **CONSIDER THE TOP FIVE RECYCLABLES.** Washing, sorting, transporting, and converting stuff back into raw materials is hard work. And it's rare for a recycled product to be exactly the same as the original material. Because of this, there's room for debate on the benefits of recycling certain things. Most of the time, though, recycling something requires less energy than manufacturing the same item from raw materials.

Keep in mind this list of the five most important things to recycle.

THE TOP FIVE RECYCLABLES

Material	Product	Why?
Aluminum	Juice cans Soda cans Aluminum foil	One of the most efficient materials, aluminum is 100 percent recyclable.
Glass Containers	Clear, amber, or emerald bottles and jars	Glass can be recycled indefinitely with essentially no loss in quality or purity.
Paper	Newspaper Magazines Scrap paper Envelopes Paperboard Cardboard	Paper comprises a third of all the municipal waste stream; it can be recycled up to seven times before it must be discarded.
Steel	Auto parts Appliances Cutlery	Any grade of steel can be recycled to top-quality new metal.
Plastic Containers (PET and HDPE)	Water bottles Detergent bottles Shampoo bottles Milk jugs	Making plastic out of recycled resources uses about two-thirds less energy than making new plastic.

DOCUMENT IT

The Concept of Zero Waste

```
MAKE A LIST OF THINGS
THAT, FROM NOW ON,
YOU CAN DO WITHOUT
```

Critics argue that upcycling, repurposing, and recycling merely postpone the inevitable—a soaring worldwide trash crisis—and that these small steps alone are not enough. It's true, all garbage eventually winds up in landfills. Inherent in the understanding of upcycling, repurposing, and recycling, however, is the utopian concept of zero waste—a completely trash-free life. This is the ultimate challenge, based on the idea that it's best to reduce your waste at the start than to revive waste after it is generated. Consider products that you will no longer purchase because of environmental reasons such as heavy packaging or long-distance transportation.

———————————

Certainly, to reverse trash overflow, we need to shift our attitudes and behavior toward more sustainable lifestyles and expectations—simply buy less stuff and demand less packaging. Push your attitudes and behaviors into more sustainable routines. Lead a simpler, more self-sufficient, mostly trash-free lifestyle. Think of the Earth as an island. There is nowhere else for your stuff to go.

11

Build a Community

We are each other's harvest; we are each other's business;
we are each other's magnitude and bond.
—GWENDOLYN BROOKS

In nature, not one organism lives in simple isolation. Each individual coexists and interacts with other organisms of the same or different species. Every organism is part of a complete community of creatures, each interacting with each other as well as with its environment. Complex interrelationships—like competition, predation, and mutualism—link together different species. Healthy communities are never static—species are continually lost and replaced. There is constant change and flux. In the wild, a community is a functional unit. It is something far more powerful than the sum of its parts.

Everyday lifestyle changes can have a significant impact on your environmental footprint. Though, if we want to bring about change on a large scale—one beyond the scope of our front porches and backyards—we need to tap into a similar communal power. Change does not happen alone. We formulate thoughts, and then set them loose, running wild and weightless into the world—but not until other people snatch them up are they truly influential and powerful. In the end, environmentalism is a social movement.

Early America brims with grassroots mobilizations intended to get voices heard and needs met—tenacious pioneers driven to seek freedom from inequality, violence, tyranny, and war, and unshakable folks who built powerful communities meant to hurdle obstacles and resolve conflicts. But amid today's busy, structured lives, overcommitted schedules, and congested neighborhoods, we've lost some perspective. We're increasingly isolated and socially fragmented. And we've forgotten something completely—that resistance is built body by body from small handfuls—*communities*—of thoughtful, committed citizens.

It's time to introduce ourselves to other like-minded people, to organize groups around shared concerns, to build dynamic communities. It's time to mobilize like-minded people in support of causes, and to create a sense of belonging, a feeling that you are not alone—that you are part of something bigger than yourself.

In this chapter, you'll strengthen the communities around you—the wild ones and the personal ones. You'll continue down the purposeful path you've been on—making meaningful everyday lifestyle changes based on environmental cues—and take things just a step further. You'll bring people together for effective action, creating a community where each citizen experiences valuable lasting connections to broad-minded capable neighbors and understands that there is strength in numbers. Soon you'll see the world as a dynamic system. Nothing exists in isolation—neither you, nor an entire species, nor an environmental problem.

The Bee Coop

Solitary bee species like the ones that inhabit a simple backyard bee coop comprise 90 percent of the global bee population. Although most solitary bees live alone, some build nests in groups, or *aggregations*, when a nesting site is particularly top-notch. A handmade coop filled with solitary bees is not merely a collection of unrelated bee species living together; it is a closely knit group or society, acting as one functional unit, gathering local pollen, nectar, and building independent nests. Interactions within the community—like a bustling apartment building—create and shape it. Because they don't have a large nest with lots of offspring to defend, solitary bees are not aggressive and rarely sting, preferring to avoid people and just get to and from work. By constructing and maintaining a backyard bee coop, you create a valuable natural resource for these bees right in your own backyard. As well there is

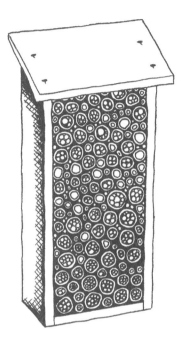

no reason to believe that the tenets of bee biology wouldn't apply to your own life. In observing their dynamic community, you may learn some important life lessons, most importantly that there is strength in numbers.

Note: *Most likely your garage or local thrift store has a wooden frame that will work for this project. Look for an old shallow, un-*

BEE COOP PROJECT MATERIALS
- HANDSAW
- HAMMER AND LONG NAILS
- TAPE MEASURE
- WOODEN FRAME
- SCRAP WOOD
- LONG STICK OR WOODEN DOWEL
- DRY HOLLOW PLANT MATERIAL OR CRAFT PAPER
- MUD

painted, chemical-free crate or drawer. It should measure 15 cm × 20 cm deep and will eventually be positioned with the drawer bottom against a wall and the shorter drawer sides on top and bottom. Alternatively, you may use scrap lumber to build a frame that measures 15 cm × 25 cm × 50 cm. A wooden back is not necessary as long as the coop is placed against a wall. If you plan to hang it from a fence post, the box will need a back.

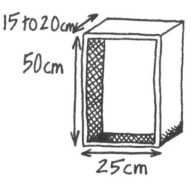

PROJECT STEPS

STEP 1. Clean the wooden frame with soap and water. Allow it to dry thoroughly.

STEP 2. Build a roof. Cut a piece of scrap wood the same width as the frame's top, but 10 cm × 20 cm deeper than the frame. Cut a wooden dowel or stick the same length as the coop frame. With the dowel underneath the scrap wood, create an angled overhanging "roof" and attach it with several long nails.

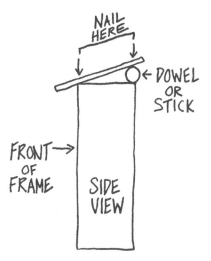

STEP 3. Gather plant material. Hollow, straight dry material is perfect for this project—bamboo canes filled with bundles of straight stalks of raspberries, Japanese knotweed, oat and wheat straw, brambles, and reeds. Think like a bug. If plant material is not within your reach, feel free to consider discarded craft or parcel paper for the job.

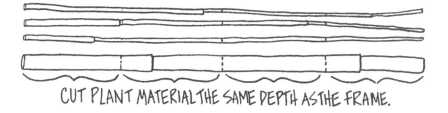

CUT PLANT MATERIAL THE SAME DEPTH AS THE FRAME.

STEP 4. Cut the plant material into segments measuring the depth of the frame. If you're using craft paper, cut pages the depth of the frame, roll them separately around pencils of different diameters, and tape each side to secure.

STEP 5. Place a handful of thick mud into a large bowl. Dip one end of each long nesting cylinder into 1 centimeter of the mud.

STEP 6. Stack the cylinders carefully mud end first within the frame, filling larger plant stalks with smaller hollow stalks or craft paper cylinders. The frame should be completely filled.

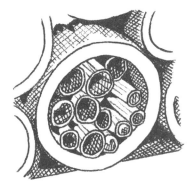

STEP 7. Mount the frame to a sunny south-facing wall or fence at least 1 meter off the ground.

STEP 8. Put out your vacancy sign. Be patient. Bees will soon start making reservations.

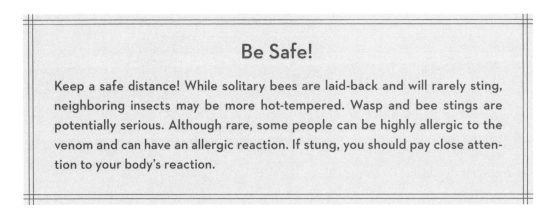

Be Safe!

Keep a safe distance! While solitary bees are laid-back and will rarely sting, neighboring insects may be more hot-tempered. Wasp and bee stings are potentially serious. Although rare, some people can be highly allergic to the venom and can have an allergic reaction. If stung, you should pay close attention to your body's reaction.

OH, THE SCIENCE OF IT ALL!

A Bee's Life

A bee coop creates a community, and holes of different sizes encourage species diversity. During spring and summer, different species of solitary bees will occupy different diameters of tubes and tunnels. Unlike bumblebees or honeybees, solitary bees don't live in colonies; they construct individual nests for their larvae. In the wild, some nest in small underground holes or tunnels or in sandy banks, piles of sand, or crumbling mortar. Others use the hollow stems of dead plants. Inside each hole, a female will provision each egg with a mixture of pollen, nectar, and saliva, and will seal the door shut. Cavities will be filled with a series of eggs. The eggs will soon hatch—each larva will eat its scrumptious snack, rapidly develop, then pupate and overwinter in a dormant state until it's ready to emerge as a perky adult bee the following spring or summer.

Bee egg-laying activity will cease by mid-September at the latest. Persistent windblown rain has the potential to cause rot and dissolve the mud walls of the nest cells. It is important to protect the bee babies within your homemade bee coop from the weather. In early fall, remove occupied cylinders and store them in a cold, dry place during the winter to protect them from harsh winter weather. An unheated shed or garage is perfect for the job. Return them to the bee coop in early spring. Young bees that have overwintered in a dormant state will emerge and start the cycle over again.

THE BEE

MOST BEES HAVE ROBUST BODIES WITH FLAT REAR LEGS. MOST ARE FUZZY AND CARRY AN ELECTROSTATIC CHARGE THAT AIDS IN POLLEN COLLECTION. MOST BEES ARE MILD MANNERED AND NON-AGGRESSIVE. FEMALES GATHER POLLEN AND NECTAR TO USE FOR THEIR FAMILIES.

THAT BUZZING SOUND YOU HEAR ON YOUR FAMILY PICNIC? PROBABLY A WASP.....

THE WASP

MOST WASPS ARE CARNIVOROUS AND HUNT FOR PREY SUCH AS OTHER INSECTS, SPIDERS, ARTHROPODS, AND CATERPILLARS, BUT SOME ALSO VISIT FLOWERS FOR NECTAR. WASPS ARE GENERALLY MORE AGGRESSIVE THAN BEES. ALMOST ALL INSECT STINGS RESULT FROM WASPS.

Befriending Bees

Scientists have recently been alarmed and puzzled by mass die-offs in worldwide bee populations. You don't have to be a professional beekeeper to help improve the current world crisis in honeybee and native bee population declines. It is easy to just be a good neighbor and help strengthen their local communities. The relative location of food, water, and cover is what creates usable insect habitat. Generally, larger areas with mixed vegetation have greater species diversity, but a well-laid-out modest backyard with a variety of food, cover, and water can entice a wide assortment of pollinators. Here are some basic steps to take.

BEE-FRIENDLY TIPS

Do Nothing	Allow half of your garden to remain unmanicured. Leave some wild, untamed messy spots in your backyard. Allow the weeds to grow up and the insects to move in. Bees don't discriminate between your prized perennials and the weeds in your lawn. By encouraging natural predators like bats, frogs, toads, spiders, birds, and ladybugs, you'll end up with fewer garden pests like aphids and slugs.
Reduce Mulch	Cut back on mulch and leave undisturbed bare soil in place whenever possible. Ground-nesting bees dig nests in the soil, and a layer of mulch discourages them from nesting. Leave a few sunny mulch-free plant-free spots.
Leave Leaves	Leave fallen trees and leaves. Digger bees burrow underground, but prefer an entrance camouflaged with leaf litter.
Go Organic	Use compost, not chemicals. Recent studies point to common pesticides as a culprit in declining bee populations.

Boost Diversity	Reduce the size of your lawn and plant a wide variety of native long-blooming nectar-rich plants. Plant flowers of vivid diverse color that bloom successively over the spring, summer, and fall. Landscape with features that appeal to you. A bed of vibrant flowers, a shady spot under a tree, a privacy hedge, colorful fall berries, and evergreen winter shrubs are pleasing to everybody, including backyard critters.
Provide Color	Bees do not love all flowers equally. White, purple, and blue are bees' favorite colors, followed by yellow and orange. Visit local nurseries to determine appropriate species. My personal favorites are asters, goldenrod, hawthorn, *lobelia*, meadowsweet, milkweed, *spiraea*, wild geranium, *helianthus*, willow, and sneezeweed (perhaps due to the name).

EXPLORE MORE

There are concrete steps and strategies you can employ to help create powerful community organizations, like those of the bees. The trick is to find solutions to problems through close observation, innovation, and the study of real, local conditions and needs. It takes a conscious effort to survey your surroundings—and it takes sustained commitment to bring a group together for effective action. Think big even if you have to act small. The steps below will help guide you to not only become a community organizer, but a community builder.

STRENGTHEN YOUR WILD SIDE. Your simple everyday actions can have a huge positive impact on the natural communities around you. Start with someplace familiar and close—even the tiniest apartment terrace can provide adequate food and shelter for a critter. Liberate your manicured lawn—reduce the size of your grass; leave some wild, untamed areas for shelter; plant native species; and offer fresh water and nesting materials. Branches neatly stacked at a woods edge will provide years of shelter for chipmunks and rabbits. Close the ecological gap between supply and demand. Your everyday careful, deliberate actions, no matter how small, help restore neighboring communities. Improve the world through your actions. Transform your local park or backyard into a safe haven for native species. Restore it into the wildness it once was. Check these tasks off as you go.

Strengthen Your Wild Side

❏ Feed them and they will come. Plant bushes and trees with edible fruit. Often, landscape features that appeal to *you* are the same ones that appeal to birds, butterflies, and bees. Keep birdfeeders stocked during the winter. If you start, don't stop. Leave fallen leaves in place to allow birds to hunt for insects. Don't snip dead flowers. The seeds within them provide essential food for many critters.

❏ Make everybody feel welcome. Add a birdhouse designed for the beneficial birds in your area. Add a birdbath. Birds need a dependable supply of fresh, clean water for drinking and bathing. The best birdbaths mimic nature—gently sloping, shallow, and shady at ground level. Change the water once a week. Add a bat house. A colony of seven bats can consume ten thousand insects per night.

❑ Provide nesting material. Leave fallen leaves and twigs unraked. Provide backyard nooks and crannies for future nests. Stash nesting material in tree crevices, berry baskets, or mesh bags—natural materials like dry grass, straw, pet fur, sheep wool, feathers, bark strips, pine needles, small sticks and twigs, or man-made materials like yarn, string, and thin strips of cloth.

❑ Add a roost box. Birds only nest during the spring and summer months. Overwintering birds often snuggle together in large nesting cavities during colder months.

❑ Reduce the size of your lawn. Cut grass is like a desert to a wild animal. Instead, plant a wide variety of flowering native plants to attract beneficial insects such as ladybugs, ground beetles, rove beetles, lacewings, and praying mantises. Choose long-blooming, nectar-rich flowers and plants that bloom at different parts of the season.

❑ Leave dead and dying trees alone whenever possible.

❑ Avoid disturbing spiders and destroying their webs.

❑ Build up vegetation around pond edges to attract frogs and toads.

MAKE A FRIEND. Thinking that the world around you is not as you think it should be and you want to do something about it? Feeling isolated and alone in your thoughts? Longing for connection? Don't sit around and wait for somebody to bump into you. Get up and introduce yourself. Reach out and expand your group. Fill out this name tag to get things started.

TAKE BIG STEPS. Has something changed in the world that you can't ignore? Want to build a strong dynamic community to brainstorm possible solutions? Want to get your voice heard and needs met? There are concrete steps and strategies you can employ to help you create a powerful community organization.

COMMUNITY-BUILDING STEPS

Do Your Research	Think of something important to you that needs fixing. Start small—like a school garden that remains unused and overgrown, or a local stream that suffers from overfishing. Consider redesigning something that has been carelessly designed. Ask important questions.

Develop a Vision	Paint a picture in your mind of how you envision the future. What are your objectives? What are your dreams? Brainstorm.
Craft a Message	Put your idea into writing. Tell the whole story. Don't let fears of regulations or constraints get in the way.
Advertise	Attract interest from potential community members. Use your charm.
Be Inclusive	No single philosophy can solve all the world's problems. Listen to others. Don't be too selective. People will surprise you with their talents. The more varied the support, the more important and universal your movement will be.
Get Comfy	Provide the means to get to know each other. Create a comfortable space where everyone's voice can be equally heard.
Lead by Example	Organize the group. Focus on gifts and talents and capabilities. Be actively involved.
Get to Work	Establish your group's principles and develop strategies to realize the goals.
Get Out There	Your community's success will depend on how securely it adheres to all sectors of society. If it's absorbed into existing institutions, it will most likely help shift society's way of thinking.

DOCUMENT IT

Join Forces

There is power in leaving your perspective where somebody else can come across it. Create a community. Start a local hiking club, organize a tree-planting day, host a garden-grown potluck dinner—get started with just a smidgen of encouragement. Your small idea could snowball into a big event.

Make a poster of your plan and pin it up someplace highly visible.

SPREAD THE WORD

It's true that we have more power than we realize to strengthen communities and make lasting changes in our world. Community organizations offer the promise of belonging, they call for us to acknowledge our interdependence, and they organize active members to do what they cannot do by themselves. The source of our current complicated ecological crisis cannot be traced back to one simple causation—and so, it will not be a quick fix. The solutions are complex and deep, and sometimes they lie in strengthening the communities around you.

12

Scatter Some Seeds

*It's the little things citizens do. That's what will make
the difference. My little thing is planting trees.*
—WANGARI MAATHAI

And so, here you are, filled with curiosity and amazement.
You've messed around with original ideas, looked at the
world from different perspectives, ventured outside to get good and
dirty, found yourself deep within the big picture of the world, sought
out inspiration from nature, harvested things you've thoughtfully grown,
shifted your attitude to a more sustainable lifestyle, introduced yourself to
others, and recognized the sheer genius of the natural world. You have
what it takes to reconnect with nature. You're a practiced pioneer—
equipped to forge your own path through our progressively more complicated frontier. Are you ready?

Now is the time to take the new things you know and put them to work.
Right now. An avalanche of unprecedented global challenges looms before
us and very few people are paying attention. How can one single individual make a difference when the Earth's problems loom so large? Here's
how: you take the information you've gathered and then share whatever

you have with the world. Everyone has something to offer. Seek out others who need help, know what you can do, and show that you can do it. Be intentional. Share creatively. Do more with less. Whatever your circumstances, your time, ideas, and unique skills can have a positive influence on the world around you. The trick is to know what you can do and be willing to do it.

Each day, what you do matters. A big ruckus can be generated from a simple purposeful act—a little thing, like scattering small seeds—made by someone just like you. An idea or behavior can move through the world like toe tapping at a scat-singing convention, starting with just a few *pit-a-pats* of an idea, and spreading rapidly out of control. You don't need to spend two years among the branches of a fifteen-hundred-year-old California redwood tree protesting its destruction to spread lasting change on a deep level. You don't need to participate in a clothing-optional protest bike ride to get your point across. You can just be you. Maybe this book is your *skeep-beep de bop-bop beep bop bo-skeedle* and your toes are tapping dangerously fast. Maybe this book is like a small magic pebble you've happened upon. Maybe your awe-inspiring superpowers are your everyday actions. Maybe your voice is your weapon, your thoughts the ammunition.

We are faced today with massive problems—environmental, social, and personal. In this chapter, you'll learn that each of us is capable of thoughtful direct actions, and we usually greatly underestimate our abilities. We all have something to say. We all have feet to move. We can all give something of ourselves. We all have seeds to scatter. That's how great rolling prairies of ideas are grown.

Handmade Seedbombs

One way to get started spreading the word is to transform a familiar spot into verdant green space. Even the smallest space can become a nature sanctuary for a teeny somebody—converted from a barren desert of concrete, manicured grass, or exotic ornamental plants into a rich dynamic native ecosystem. Seedbombs, magical little fistfuls of compacted clay, compost, and native perennial wildflower seed, can help make this happen. Whip them up and covertly throw them into orphaned neighborhood spots. Over time, they'll break down and *abracadabra!* Native plants will sprout up in place of dirt, weeds, and invasive species. Transform neglected land into green space. Toss some seedbombs out into the world.

Note: *To determine native plant species in your area, ask a botanist, local garden center expert, or smart butterfly. Small seeds work best for seedbombs. My seedbombs include (among other seeds) eastern red columbine, red milkweed, butterfly weed, New England aster, joe-pye weed, lanceleaf coreopsis, blazing star, wild bergamot, sweet coneflower, and rigid goldenrod—all Northeastern U.S. species. Select low-maintenance drought-tolerant native species that can thrive with intermittent care. Consider*

SEEDBOMB RECIPE
- 3 PARTS CLAY
- 3 PARTS SOIL
- 1 PART SMALL NATIVE PERENNIAL SEED
- 1 TO 2 PARTS WATER (ADDED IN SMALL AMOUNTS)
- BUCKET AND SHOVEL
- BAKING SHEET
- NEWSPAPER

The Soil Squeeze Test

Take a handful of moist (but not wet) soil from the spot you'd like to spruce up and give it a firm squeeze. When you open your hand, one of three things will happen. Test your soil and fill in the corresponding oval.

1. The soil falls apart as soon as you open your hand. This means you have *sandy* soil.
2. The soil holds its shape, and when you give it a little poke, it crumbles. This means you have *loam*. Perfect for a garden—your soil retains moisture and nutrients, but doesn't stay soggy.
3. The soil holds it shape, and when you give it a little poke, it sits stubbornly in your hand. This means you have nutrient-rich *clay* soil. Perfect for this project.

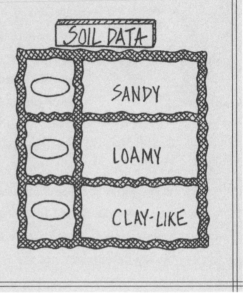

species that create habitats for other native critters like butterflies and birds. Choose your seeds wisely. You certainly do not want to select invasive species that will threaten biodiversity.

PROJECT STEPS

STEP 1. Gather ingredients and head outside with them. Be prepared to get dirty.

STEP 2. To determine your soil type, do the squeeze test. If you have heavy clay soil, you are in luck since there will be no need for clay amendment in your seedbomb recipe. Just head to your orphaned plot of land and collect a bucket of soil. If your soil is sandy or loamy, however, you will need to add natural clay, terracotta clay powder, or air-dry clay (found in stream banks, health food stores, or art supply shops).

STEP 3. Like making a mudpie, making a seedbomb is not an exact science. Use the recipe as a guide, but measurements needn't be exact. If your soil is clay-like, omit the clay in the recipe. The mixture should be moist, but not wet. Knead it with your hands, being sure to incorporate all seeds. Roll it into 2- to 5-centimeter balls. Set them on a newspaper-lined baking sheet by a sunny window to dry for two days before using.

STEP 4. Nicely packaged in a teeny bag, seedbombs make fantastic handmade gifts for friends, family, and deserving cello teachers. Include directions and a nice note or quote.

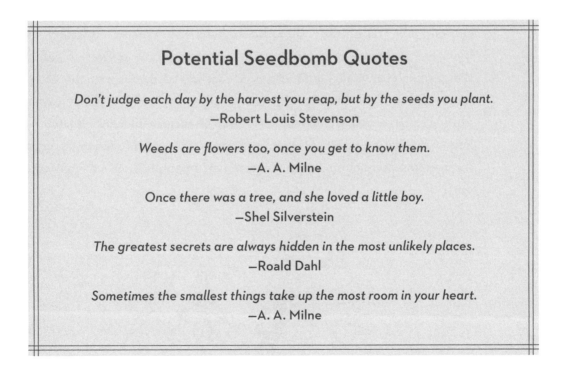

Potential Seedbomb Quotes

Don't judge each day by the harvest you reap, but by the seeds you plant.
—Robert Louis Stevenson

Weeds are flowers too, once you get to know them.
—A. A. Milne

Once there was a tree, and she loved a little boy.
—Shel Silverstein

The greatest secrets are always hidden in the most unlikely places.
—Roald Dahl

Sometimes the smallest things take up the most room in your heart.
—A. A. Milne

STEP 5. Your seedbombs are ready to wreak havoc on green wastelands. Keep in mind that seed germination is highly dependent on water. Watch the weather. To ensure germination, scatter the seedbombs on the ground—or toss over a fence onto an empty lot—right before an early spring rainy spell. Then, just throw and they will grow. Rich in nutrients, the clay and compost aid in germination and help strengthen plant root systems.

Now, go scatter some seeds already!

OH, THE SCIENCE OF IT ALL!

Invasive Species

If you are a microscopic spiny water flea minding your own business devouring zooplankton, you might be surprised one day to find yourself sucked into a transoceanic ship's ballast tank and transported from your Black Sea birthplace to a brand-new home in Lake Ontario. Once released there, you may be delighted to discover that you easily outcompete native larval fish for food—consuming twenty daphnia each day. Yay! But, if you are a little larval lake trout, a native to Lake Ontario, you may be heartbroken to find that a peppy new neighbor has moved in and is decimating your zooplankton population. Sadly, you sleep on an empty stomach from now on. Drat.

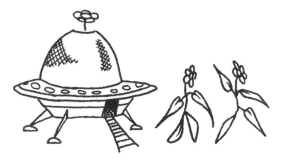

An *exotic*, or *alien*, species is any organism introduced into an area where it's not naturally found. Many nonnative plants have established themselves in brand-new habitats and eventually outcompete native species for resources—these are *invasive species*. You may not realize it, but these surround you—the house sparrow, brown rat, starling, bullfrog, Asian carp, zebra mussel, Japanese beetle, stinkbug, red imported fire ant, common reed, burning bush—their accidental or intentional introduction into new habitats took native species completely by evolutionary surprise. Freed from their natural predators, pathogens, parasites, and competitors, invasive species drastically change the native ecosystem and threaten or endanger organisms. There are exotic extremes like kudzu, a perennial plant native to Japan that was introduced to the southern United States as a forage crop and ornamental plant. Growing as much as a half meter per day, it now covers seven million acres in a dense tangle of vines that scramble up and over any fixed object—trees, telephone poles, barns, and parked vehicles. It's been nicknamed "the vine that ate the South."

Verify that the seeds and plants you're putting in the ground are not invasive. Jot down a dependable list of potential native plants to put in. Scatter seeds with a clear conscience.

➸ NOW TRY THIS ➸

Guerrilla Gardening

Unbeknownst to you perhaps, there is a (slightly) unlawful silent underground movement popping up all around us. Guerrilla gardening is the unauthorized cultivation of plants on otherwise neglected public or private land in response to dwindling green space. One part beautification, one part eco-activism, it's a burgeoning crusade. The idea is to reclaim green space, regardless of who actually owns it. Technically, guerrilla gardening is illegal. You must accept the fact that some folks might view it as vandalism, just performed with plants instead of spray paint, rocks, or eggs. Guerrilla gardening is more than just planting. It's putting green where it's not expected—it's putting something common in an unusual place or something uncommon in a usual place—it's surprising people and making them reevaluate their position in the natural world.

It's time to plan a clandestine small-scale planting attack in a neglected neighborhood area—to take back orphaned land all but forgotten—to reclaim green space. It's time to be a free-range planter on a mission. It's time to make a ruckus without anyone's permission.

What should you plant? If possible, find a generous gardening friend with a good native plant or seed selection. Otherwise, purchase things from a local nursery or seed supplier. Select low-maintenance drought-tolerant local species that can thrive with intermittent care. Choose perennial species wisely. You certainly do not want to

Possible Planting Options

Select one or more:

- **Bulbs:** Usually planted in the fall, these shrimpy storehouses are simple to plant and they arise as a spring surprise.
- **Perennial plants, shrubs, and trees:** Just pop in a plant. Choose a hardy, preferably perennial native plant that is easy to maintain. It should live for two or more years.
- **Annual plants with big "wow" factor:** Choose something that will catch someone's eye—a plant with a powerful punch.
- **Classic clay seedbombs:** These little nuggets are used to surreptitiously improve areas that a guerrilla gardener is unable to reach. Locked vacant lots or roadside embankments—all are promising native plant nurseries.

select invasive perennials that will threaten biodiversity. Consider species that create habitats for other critters.

As for where to plant, look around and consider a few unloved orphaned spots close to home—empty pots or concrete planters, abandoned public gardens, vacant parking lots—even a gap in pavement can serve as a modest blank canvas.

One quick note: *I don't advocate tossing squash seeds or planting petunias in your neighbor's weedy flower bed, and certainly I don't suggest planting a community garden or tree farm on the sly. Just one or two plants will do for now. You need a sunny spot and good soil. In fact, a portable pot placed near a street sign or next to the town barber's door may be the ideal start to a career of gardening with intention. Of course, you should sneak by to water it every so often, or leave with it an encouraging sign. Never underestimate the power of a plant. It doesn't need a cape or spandex to change the world.*

EXPLORE MORE

There are other ways to scatter seeds and improve the world through your actions. Just a tiny input from you is enough to get started, and things will gather momentum. Ideas and behaviors spread rapidly through a crowd like contagious laughter. Doing one or two small things can spark a radical movement. Start a positive epidemic of your own. Here are other ways to make a difference.

MAIL SOMETHING TO SOMEBODY BIG. Sometimes you can spread seeds with words. Your brain is full of electrifying ideas that might spark a change in somebody else's way of looking at things. Think about something that moves you. Do some research and get the lowdown on the history of the issue. Locate a local governmental committee or elected official—environmental conservation board, town mayor, state senator—and start writing. Keep your note brief. A short letter is good. Introduce yourself. Then, start with your strongest point. Keep a positive tone. Be nice. No yelling. Represent other viewpoints in the most favorable light possible. Don't present a distorted picture. Then, present your case and back yourself up. Ask them to take action. Thank them. And then thank them again.

CRAFT A STATEMENT. With our complex global problems, there's room for a wide range of initiatives and actions to raise public awareness. Symbolic gestures—political, heartwarming, or funny—can be powerful and effective methods for change. Tune in to your creative side and craft a statement of your own. Be a drive-by knitter, a nameless needleworker, a clandestine quilter—and model artful forms of civic engagement in public spots. Or plan a participatory public project—a spontaneous community bike ride or neighborhood kite-flying crusade—to raise awareness of things

DEAR _____,

   HELLO. I AM WRITING REGARDING
_____,

AND TO EXPRESS MY CONCERN ABOUT_____

_____,

AND ESPECIALLY_____

_____.

   I UNDERSTAND THAT THERE ARE
MULTIPLE PERSPECTIVES CONCERNING THIS
ISSUE. I AM PLEASED TO SEE_____

_____.

THIS IS IMPORTANT. HOWEVER, I AM
CONCERNED ABOUT _____

_____

AND I CAN'T HELP THINKING THAT_____

_____.

   THE BEST SOLUTION WOULD BE TO_____

_____.

THIS WOULD HELP_____,
PLEASE CONSIDER _____

_____.

   THANK YOU FOR TAKING THE TIME TO
CONSIDER MY SUGGESTIONS. I LOOK
FORWARD TO HEARING BACK FROM YOU.

SINCERELY,

_____

A CONCERNED CITIZEN

that matter. Keep in mind that the goal is to get people to start talking—and keep talking—about things you consider important.

DOCUMENT IT

A Truehearted Pioneer

Don't get overwhelmed with looming environmental threats—anyone can bring about lasting change. Just take it one step, one action, one word at a time. If you find that nobody's listening to you, be loud. Make some noise. Don't wait for your turn to talk.

You are a tough pioneer that can spur dramatic and fast societal change. You alone are enough to raise awareness and inspire others to join in. Don't worry if you start off alone on your trek across the rugged frontier. Just start bushwhacking solo. Although at first you may be uncertain and lonely, others will catch up shortly. You'll soon find what you're looking for—the old backcountry buried deep beneath roads, strip malls, and newspaper piles. Before long, in the blaze of spring flowers and the solitude of wilderness, you'll watch your homestead grow.

Use the following checklist to be certain you're heading in the right direction.

Checklist for a Truehearted Pioneer

- ❏ Mess around with original ideas

- ❏ Eat lower on the food chain

- ❏ Think like a minimalist

- ❏ Line-dry your laundry

- ❏ Think for yourself

- ❏ Spend quality time outside

- ❏ Walk, ride your bike, carpool, or roller-skate

- ❏ Consider the lifespan of objects you buy

- ❏ Plant and harvest something

- ❏ Support your local farmers' market

- ❏ Be aware of the wider world around you

- ❏ Write an important letter to an important person

- ❏ Fill up your recycling bin to the top

- ❏ Reuse scrap paper; recycle newspaper

- ❏ Slow down and let things sink in

- ❏ Use public transportation

- ❏ Eat seasonal food

- ❏ Reduce your consumption

- ❏ Spread the word

So, here we stand at the final chapter's very end, and there are so many other things I wanted to tell you. It's been said that endings are the saddest part. Deep in our hearts we know, though, that the best things always come last. We could sit and talk for hours and hours about very important things, but in the end it is the final words that linger on. And, in this case, the words are this:

Go scatter some seeds.

BE THE RIVER

MOVE. JUST MOVE.
DON'T LET THE WORLD LOOK PAST YOU.
BE THE SNOWDROP IN SNOW.
BE THE WEED SPROUTING FROM THE STONE.
BE THE VOICE.
BE THE MUSIC.
BE THE CORAL SNAKE, THE ECHO, THE TETHER, THE STORY.
BE THE WISHBONE, THE OPEN BOOK.
BE THE BREATH.
BE THE LIFE.
BE THE EARTHQUAKE, THE FEATHER, THE KNIFE.
BE THE STUBBORN SPOT.
BE THE BEST IDEA YOU'VE EVER HAD.
BE THE CURIOUS CHILD.
BE THE CYCLONE.
BE THE RIVER.

DON'T WAIT FOR YOUR TURN.
BE THE CURTAIN RISING.
STAND UP.
YELL AND BE HEARD.
TODAY, BE AMAZING.
AND THEN,

BE THE OCEAN.

Acknowledgments

It's a peculiar thing that my name stands all alone on the cover of this book. As much as I'd like to take credit as a champion who single-handedly cranked out the preceding pages, a marvelous team effort has launched this book into the world.

First and foremost, I am so fortunate to have Perigee as my publisher, specifically my superstar editor, Meg Leder. Her enthusiasm, patience, thoughtful reads, and all-around good sense were invaluable. Her sharp eye and passion for great writing is evident in every page. A thousand thank-yous, Meg. I also offer deep thanks to the book's creative team and behind-the-scenes Penguin Random House folks. They were so much more that just mysterious people who scanned sketches and checked my subject-verb agreement. They graciously welcomed my ideas about page layout, chapter artwork, and cover design, and composed pages that read clearly and flow well.

This whole endeavor was set into motion by my friend and neighbor

Robin Dellabough, whose encouragement and ardent passion for creativity are an inspiration. Not only did Robin plant the seed for the project, but she believed in me from the very first word, stumbled patiently through really awkward first proposal versions, and introduced me to my literary agent, Lisa DiMona. I am forever indebted to Lisa, who knew before even I did that this was the book I should be writing, and offered me invaluable strategic guidance and support. Without Lisa's diligent efforts, both during the original writing and editing of the chapters and throughout the book's assembly, I would be just another restless school garden coordinator felting wool and writing sporadic blog posts. Thank you as well to Jenny Rosenstrach, who encouraged me to write the blog that sparked the idea for this book. Her sympathetic ear and thoughtful suggestions offered along the way were a tremendous help.

Although more than twenty years have passed, I still feel it's essential to thank Ellen Ketterson and the late Val Nolan Jr. at Indiana University, both of whom sent me walking alone on remote southern Appalachian trails in search of dark-eyed junco nests, sparking within me a deep and continued interest in ecology. And thanks to Maud Fluchere, neighbor gardener extraordinaire, for entrusting me years ago with wheelbarrowfuls of her divided bulbs and perennials when my garden was just a lump of weeds. They're still going strong, Maud.

A special thank-you to Sue and Jim Chambers, my mom and dad, who encouraged my lifelong love affair with all creatures big and small, and taught me to select a quality hammer, to watch the telltales, and to end everything with a half hitch. The enduring warmth of their friendship has remained a touchstone of my life and has shaped me in profound ways. Thank you to my brother, Scott Chambers, and his family, and to my in-laws, Helen and David Cuff. I've read all but just a few of the newspaper clippings sent to me.

Thanks to Arrington Kitchin Carr, Ian Carr, Todd Lawlor, and Anne Scharer, whose enthusiastic participation in this project (and in my life!) has been essential. Faithful friends and all-around great folks—they provided timely advice over cheap wine and home-cooked meals, and put gloppy embryonic versions of "Buzz Off!" Bug Lotion to the test in extreme camping conditions. Gratitude doesn't begin to describe it.

Thank you to friends in my hometown and beyond who put up with me while I was writing, whether by staying close by, staying tactfully away, or taking time to read the manuscript: Toby Adams, Amy Butler, Melanie Choukas-Bradley, Jeff Gordinier, Adrian Higgins, Holli Howard, Catherine Kelley, Ellen Ketterson, Annie Leonard, Richard Louv, Charlotte Lyons, Bill McKibben, Michael Petrula, Bernadette Noll, M. Sanjayan, David Yarnold, the Fabulous Rivertowns Bloggers, and the Artisans Gallery Gals. Thank you to Sammy Wright, who lived in full belief that we can all make a difference in the world. Thank you to my smallish friends—Anna, James, Madeline, Evan, Aengus, Eoin, Lulu, Maxine, Hazel, and all of the Dows Lane Garden students—every day they remind me to slow down and feel the moment of now. And to the hundreds of people who have commented on my blog posts with such heart. It's hard to overstate how much that feedback has affected me. I am forever appreciative.

Thank you to my girls, Syd and Mary (listed respectfully in foot size order), who amaze me every day with their insightful questions and inspirational ideas, and remind me, when I have all but forgotten, what life is really all about. Holding their hands in mine is both an honor and a privilege.

And finally, I am infinitely grateful for my husband, Brian Cuff—my friend for a quarter of a century and favorite person of all time—who picked up the slack and provided consistent support, encouragement, clarity, and humor throughout this whole thing, and continues to wow me every single day. Without him there would just be no point.

About the Author

Marcie Cuff lives just north of Manhattan with her husband and two young daughters. With an MA in secondary science teaching and a background in evolutionary biology and studio art, her professional experience is a mix of studio art and the natural sciences. She has lived as an organic lettuce farmer, a tropical rainforest field technician, an Alaskan tent-dwelling graduate student, a stuffed animal designer, a Manhattan high school biology teacher, and an elementary school garden coordinator. Now a nature columnist for a regional newspaper the *Hudson Independent*, she has written professionally for a large part of her life. Her blog *Mossy* is devoted to families who share a love of slowing down, simplifying, getting dirty, and finding hands-on connections to art and nature. Find out more on her website, marciecuff.com.

Come grow with me! Be part of a BRANCH!

For information about organizing or joining book groups
based on *This Book Was a Tree*, visit marciecuff.com.

CALLING ALL MODERN PIONEERS!

We live in a spectacular time of unprecedented digital connectivity. Yet never before have we been so disconnected from the natural world. It's time to remedy this—to roll up our sleeves and explore a world of unsurpassed beauty and possibility.

With *This Book Was a Tree*, you'll decipher nature's perplexing puzzles through messy but purposeful projects—felting wool, making seedbombs, assembling a nature junk journal, maintaining an herb garden, constructing a bee coop, and germinating nutritious edible sprouts. Along the way, you'll uncover curious details and intriguing similarities between your life and those of your feathered, furry, and flying neighbors, and reawaken your raw sense of wonder and imagination.

Think of this as your guidebook for becoming a modern pioneer—a strong-minded, clever, crafty, spontaneous, mud pie–making, fort-building individual committed to slowing down and giving the world your complete attention, questioning everyday things, and reconnecting with the wildness around you.

MARCIE CHAMBERS CUFF is a nature columnist for the *Hudson Independent* and runs *Mossy*, a blog highlighting innovative family projects and hands-on parenting commentary. She works as a garden coordinator at a local elementary school and organizes and maintains a community-based vegetable garden. For more information, see MossyMossy.com.

CRAFTS/HOBBIES
penguin.com

U.S. $16.00
CAN $18.00

T2-EDM-645